THE SOVIET AIR FORCE AT WAR

TIME LIFE® BOOKS

Other Publications:

THE CIVIL WAR
PLANET EARTH
COLLECTOR'S LIBRARY OF THE CIVIL WAR
LIBRARY OF HEALTH
CLASSICS OF THE OLD WEST
THE GOOD COOK
THE SEAFARERS
WORLD WAR II
HOME REPAIR AND IMPROVEMENT
THE OLD WEST
LIFE LIBRARY OF PHOTOGRAPHY (revised)
LIFE SCIENCE LIBRARY (revised)

For information on and a full description of any of the Time-Life
Books series listed above, please write:
Reader Information
Time-Life Books
541 North Fairbanks Court
Chicago, Illinois 60611

*This volume is one of a series that traces the adventure and
science of aviation from the earliest manned balloon ascension
through the era of jet flight.*

THE SOVIET AIR FORCE AT WAR

by Russell Miller

AND THE EDITORS OF TIME-LIFE BOOKS

TIME-LIFE BOOKS, ALEXANDRIA, VIRGINIA

THE AUTHOR

Russell Miller is a British journalist and freelance writer who frequently contributes to *The Sunday Times* of London. He is the author of four previous Time-Life books, among them *The Commandos* for the World War II series and *Continents in Collision* for the Planet Earth series.

THE CONSULTANTS

Von Hardesty is an Associate Curator in the Department of Aeronautics, National Air and Space Museum, Smithsonian Institution. Previously he taught European and Russian history at Ohio Wesleyan University and Blufton College. A specialist in Soviet air power, he is the author of *Red Phoenix,* a definitive history of the Soviet Air Force.

Dr. John Greenwood, Chief Historian of the United States Army Corps of Engineers, holds a Ph.D. in military and Soviet history from Kansas State University. He has written extensively on both the Soviet and United States Air Forces.

Alexander Boyd is a former director of Defense Studies at the Royal Air Force Staff College. A lecturer in Russian history and literature, he has published *The Soviet Air Force since 1918* and collaborated on two studies of the Soviets and their air strategy.

Library of Congress Cataloguing in Publication Data
Miller, Russell.
    The Soviet Air Force at war.
    (The Epic of flight)
    Bibliography: p.
    Includes index.
    1. Aeronautics, Military—Soviet Union—History.
I. Time-Life Books.   II. Title.   III. Series.
UG635.S65M54 1983   358.4'00947   83-9105
ISBN 0-8094-3371-0 (lib. bdg.)

CONTENTS

ДА ЗДРАВСТВУЮТ СОВЕТСКИЕ ЛЕТЧИКИ-ГОРД

With a wave and a smile, Soviet leader Joseph Stalin and
Defense Commissar Kliment E. Voroshilov salute an Aviation Day
formation of bombers and fighter planes as it roars over Red
Square in Moscow. The 1938 poster proclaims: "Long Live Soviet
Pilots, Proud Falcons of Our Motherland."

СОКОЛЫ НАШЕЙ РОДИНЫ!

The celebration of Communist flight

On August 18, 1937, nearly one million Russian citizens made their way to Tushino Airfield—by train, by bus, by truck and on foot—to view an exhibition of aircraft, the most highly touted product of Soviet industry and the proudest arm of Soviet military might. Russian factories had produced 4,435 airplanes that year, and Muscovites were being given a chance this day to see the Red Air Force put the craft through maneuvers. The show was dazzling; its climax came when dozens of planes moved gracefully in and out of formations that spelled LENIN, STALIN and USSR and then, for a grand finale, took the shape of a five-pointed star, symbol of the Bolshevik Revolution.

No one needed to make a pilgrimage to Moscow that year, or any other, to perceive that aviation was a prime manifestation of Communism's success. In major cities throughout the vast land, aerial exhibitions dominated the public observances of major holidays, including May Day and the anniversary of the Bolshevik Revolution on November 7; there was even a special Aviation Day on August 18. And holiday or no, Russians had constant reminders of Soviet air power before their eyes in the form of great posters—some of them 5 by 10 feet in size and stenciled in 15 to 20 eye-catching colors—that papered the walls of railroad stations, post offices, schools, hospitals, factories and farm buildings everywhere.

After 1941, when the Soviets were engulfed in the desperate conflict known to them then and now as the Great Patriotic War, the posters celebrating the Air Force took on an ever greater importance. For here was the shield and far-reaching sword of the embattled Red Army. In Moscow, a special government section employed artists to draw hundreds of Air Force posters that were printed in uncounted millions. And as the War progressed, the posters' tone gradually changed from one of grim and implacable defiance to a lusty roar of victory.

ДА ЗДРАВСТВУЮТ СОВЕТСКИЕ ЛЕТЧИКИ, ГОРДЫЕ СОКОЛЫ НАШЕЙ РОДИНЫ!

Three bemedaled Soviet pilots line up for review under a skyful of transport planes and a giant portrait of Stalin in a poster that reiterates, "Long Live Soviet Pilots." Stalin made much of the nation's fliers and decorated them with the Soviet Union's highest awards.

ДА ЗДРАВСТВУЕТ МОГУЧАЯ АВИАЦИЯ
СТРАНЫ СОЦИАЛИЗМА!

СЛАВА ГЕРОЯМ ОТЕЧЕСТВЕННОЙ ВОЙНЫ! СЛАВА СТАЛИНСКИМ СОКОЛАМ!

Amidst a swarm of diving fighters, a begoggled Soviet flier mans his machine gun in 1941, when the Soviets were starting their counteroffensives against the German invasion. "Glory to the Heroes of the Patriotic War—Glory to Stalin's Falcons" reads the legend.

СЛАВА СОВЕТСКОМУ ВОЗДУШНОМУ ФЛОТУ!

In a poster proclaiming "Glory to the Soviet Air Force," stylized Soviet fighters and bombers sweep triumphantly over a field of downed Nazi planes and burning tanks. The poster appeared in the summer of 1943, just after the Battle of Kursk, when the Soviet Air Force finally gained an edge against the Germans.

"Stalin's Falcons Are Destroying the Enemy" cries a poster depicting a Nazi vulture caught between converging Soviet planes aloft and Soviet artillery below. The poster appeared in 1942, as the Soviet forces began to thrust the Germans back.

1
The Red Falcons of Bolshevism

In the early-morning hours of July 7, 1943, a brightening blue sky and soft warm air promised a glorious summer day in the eastern Ukraine. But moments after sunrise the sky darkened as if by an immense horde of locusts. From horizon to horizon, a mighty fleet of Soviet aircraft was heading west for the Kursk salient, where German forces of more than 1,800 planes, 570,000 combat troops and 2,000 tanks were engaged in a colossal offensive meant to trap and destroy 12 Soviet armies totaling almost a million men.

During the two days that the offensive had been under way, the Germans had punched out some bloody gains. Now came the Soviet counterattack—led by the Red Air Force. The Soviet planes—emblazoned with fierce legends such as "Vengeance!" and "Death to Fascism!"—flew in perfectly orchestrated formations designed to fill the skies with the greatest possible concentration of aircraft at once.

First came squadron upon squadron of swift and deadly fighters whose mission it was to clear the sky of German interceptors. Behind them came the high-level bombers, to hammer German airfields and supply depots. Last came the ground-attack planes—the distinctively Russian Shturmoviks, humpbacked in shape and heavily plated with armor. From a cruising altitude of 2,500 feet they singled out tanks, trucks, columns of troops—anything that moved—and dropped bomb canisters that burst in midair, hurling steel fragments in every direction; then the Shturmoviks dived abruptly and came in closer on their prey, some to a terrifying 50 feet, or lower. The Shturmoviks had a bewildering repertory of tactics; one was a fearsome maneuver known as the circle of death, in which they orbited around a cluster of enemy tanks in groups of four, six or eight, delivering blasts of 37-millimeter cannon fire, 132-millimeter rockets and hollow-charge bombs that, as one Soviet flier put it, "burned holes in the fascist armor." Barely 20 minutes after the arrival of the Shturmoviks over the Wehrmacht's 9th Panzer Division on that terrible July morning, 70 enemy tanks were in flames.

The dawn attack was only a foretaste of what was to come. Behind the first wave of planes, the Soviets had thousands more to draw upon; estimates range as high as 5,400 craft, including reserves. This prodi-

Red Army airmen, the first few members of what would one day be a mighty force, stand beside a British de Havilland two-seater captured from czarist units during the Russian Civil War.

gious armada had been assembled at a complex of more than 150 airfields located within 80 miles of the front. As one unit completed its mission and peeled away to refuel and rearm, another wave swept in to take up the work. In the space of scarcely two hours, the Wehrmacht's 3rd Panzer Division lost 270 of its 300 tanks to the pitiless Shturmoviks. And a like fate befell the 17th Panzer Division, which lost 240 of its 300 tanks in four hours of desperate combat against the Red Air Force.

Throughout that day and for the next five days thereafter, the Soviet forces—planes aloft acting in teamwork with tanks and troops below—pummeled the Germans mercilessly. To Lieutenant General Pavel Rotmistrov, who stood on a hill outside the village of Prokhorovka, where his elite 5th Guards Tank Army was doing battle, it seemed that the area was "permanently in the shadow of bomber, ground-attack and fighter aircraft as one dogfight seemed to follow another without respite." A Shturmovik pilot remembered that the smoke from the burning tanks that littered the ground below "was thick and oily and as you flew through it, it seeped into your cockpit."

The Germans were thunderstruck by the onslaught. "The Russians used aircraft in numbers such as we had never yet seen in the East," said German General Horst Grossman, commander of the Westphalian 6th Infantry Division, operating north of Kursk. "The Russians are taking the steam out of our operation," said another German officer. No accurate record of comparative losses was kept, but according to one estimate, more than 1,500 Luftwaffe aircraft were destroyed in those first six days, against about 1,000 for the Soviets. More important, the toll of German tanks, trucks and artillery ran into many thousands, and the Wehrmacht dead and wounded numbered in the scores of thousands.

The awesome display of air power that blunted the German thrust in July 1943 was the culmination of an epic story of war and aviation. Just two years before, outgunned and unprepared, the Soviet air arm had itself been almost totally destroyed as a fighting force in its first encounter with the vaunted German Luftwaffe. At the end of the first week's battle, in June 1941, the Luftwaffe had demolished an astounding 4,017 Russian aircraft—nearly 60 per cent of the entire Soviet combat air strength. Vast numbers of planes had been caught helpless on the ground; pilots who did struggle aloft found that their aircraft were outmoded, their tactics amateurish and their lives in forfeit. Without air cover, the Red Army was sent reeling back in one defeat after another.

The virtual obliteration of the Red Air Force was all the more devastating because for the better part of a decade the Soviets had believed themselves possessed of the world's greatest air force. From the earliest days of the Bolshevik Revolution, Soviet authorities had seen the value of aviation, both as a symbol and arm of Communism. Aircraft had helped secure the Revolution, and in the years after, a sky filled with planes became an expression of success and modernism. Throughout more than 20 years of struggle for worldwide political legitimacy, technological proficiency and military might, the Soviets had expended enormous energy in building their air force—sometimes copying the West, occasionally leading, making flights that were truly heroic and testing their skills in distant combat.

"Aviation is the highest expression of our achievements," declared a Politburo member in 1938. The Russian public had no reason to doubt the boast. Year after year and season after season, holiday celebrations brought thousands of planes into the skies over major cities, where they put on dazzling displays of numerical force and balletic coordination.

The men who flew the aircraft were feted as heroes. Soviet leader Joseph Stalin called them his "Falcons" and personally set them the task of "flying farther than anyone, faster than anyone and higher than anyone." When the aviators responded by breaking world records for distance, speed, altitude and endurance, the press proudly called them "Bolshevik knights of culture and progress" and announced that Soviet records made "capitalist aviators pale."

Filled to bursting with so much pride, Russians could scarcely believe the debacle of the opening battle in World War II. "What was the matter with our air force?" was a question on every tongue. It was a question that no one could answer in the shock-filled days that followed. And how to recover from a catastrophe of such magnitude? The prospect seemed almost impossible. Yet the answers to both questions did come. In the space of barely two years, the Soviet Air Force rose like a phoenix from the ashes—until by mid-1943 it could exert overwhelming strength over a segment of battlefield and play a vital role in turning the tide of what every Russian called the Great Patriotic War. It was a feat without parallel in the annals of military aviation. Only a people deeply imbued with a love and knowledge of flight could have accomplished it.

The Soviet leaders might never have confessed it, but their fascination with aviation and air power was a direct legacy of the hated Czars. Imperial Russia—though it was a vast agricultural land with an outmoded feudal society—was engaged in the same quest for flight that lured men of science and industry all over the 19th Century world. Indeed, Russians like to assert that they invented the airplane. As early as 1884, a Russian naval officer by the name of Alexander Mozhaisky built a monoplane with a wingspan of about 40 feet and a slender fuselage of wood; it was powered by a steam engine imported from England. A pilot raced Mozhaisky's creation down a ramp resembling a ski jump and then glided to a landing on the ground below. Mozhaisky's invention failed to put humankind aloft. But the event clearly earned Russia a place in the chronicles of aviation.

So did some abstruse work done in the groves of Russian academe by the brilliant scientist Nikolai Zhukovsky, who, in a career that spanned four decades, wrote some 200 works on mathematics, physics and mechanics. At Zhukovsky's instigation one of the world's first wind tunnels for testing aerodynamics was built in Moscow in 1902; two years later he founded Europe's first institute of aerodynamics, and there he taught unnumbered eager students the principles of flight.

Meanwhile, in 1903, the American brothers Orville and Wilbur Wright achieved the miracle of flight over the sand dunes of Kitty Hawk, North Carolina. After news of this feat reached Russia, a motley assortment of scholars, tinkerers and gentlemen sportsmen began trying to fly. The All-Russia Aero Club was founded with the imperial imprimatur in St. Petersburg in 1908, and soon clubs like it sprang up in Moscow and Kiev and elsewhere. Such clubs invited foreign aviators to come and lecture; and their own members, still lacking planes, tasted the exhilaration of soaring in the air by means of windborne gliders.

Aviation soon passed from academe and the world of sport to the military—thanks to the quick insight of a member of the Russian Royal Family. On reading the news in a morning paper in 1909 that the French sportsman Louis Blériot had made history by flying across the English Channel, the Grand Duke Alexander Mikhailovich was instantly seized with the thought that "the country that first possesses an aerial fleet will be victorious in any future war." He expressed this notion to his brother-in-law Czar Nicholas II in the presence of the imperial ministers. "Nicky smiled," the Grand Duke recalled. "The Minister of the Navy thought I was crazy. The Minister of War, General Sukhomlinov, shook with laughter." Nevertheless, the Czar acquiesced in the purchase of a few aircraft from Gabriel and Charles Voisin, two Parisian brothers who built custom planes for Blériot and other wealthy sportsmen. The imperial government had taken a step toward building an air force.

Needing men to staff such a force, the Grand Duke also sent a corps of promising officers to Paris to take flying lessons. The following summer, the Imperial All-Russia Aero Club treated the public to a gala Aviation Week. Hundreds of Russian citizens had their first glimpse of machine-powered craft actually flying. "People gasped and cheered," the Grand Duke wrote. Toward the end of the year, the Grand Duke laid the cornerstone for an aviation school in Sevastopol, and another was founded at Gatchina, just outside St. Petersburg. Many young officers were soon clamoring to enroll for the courses.

At the same time, Russia also ventured into industry. In 1909 an aircraft factory opened in St. Petersburg; others followed in Moscow, Riga and Kiev. By 1914 Russia had seven factories turning out 30 to 40 planes a month; the largest, the Dux Works in Moscow, produced 190 planes in that year alone. Those impressive figures, however, concealed a basic weakness. The craft were of foreign design, mostly French Voisins, Nieuports, Moranes and Farmans. All were produced under licensed arrangement with foreign firms, whose owners generally provided the capital and frequently the technicians as well. And all the planes were powered by imported engines—British Sunbeam, Bristol, Vickers and Sommer; Italian Anzani; German Argus; French Gnôme.

One factory, and one alone, was successfully producing original and innovative craft. The factory was the Russo-Baltic Railcar Factory (so called because it had begun as a manufacturer of railroad cars) and the native designer was the pioneering young Igor Sikorsky.

Sikorsky, who was born the son of a prosperous physician in May 1889, showed an interest in flying as a boy of 12, when he built a small helicopter, powered by rubber bands, that could hop into the air. In 1912, when he was 22, he entered a contest in Moscow with a far more sophisticated craft—a biplane that could fly at the dizzying speed of 70 miles an hour. The plane won first prize. It also won Sikorsky a job offer from the Russo-Baltic Railcar Factory, which was headed by Mikhail Shidlovsky, a former naval officer and member of the Czar's Treasury. Besides buying the winning plane, Shidlovsky bought the rights to all of Sikorsky's designs for the next five years. He also gave Sikorsky a highly

Nikolai Zhukovsky, the father of Russian aviation, stands inside the wind tunnel of the Moscow Higher Technical School in 1914. Builder of the first such experimental device in Russia, aerodynamicist Zhukovsky authored a landmark theory showing how a wing's shape creates lift and how to calculate the amount for any wing design.

gratifying bonus, the freedom to experiment at company expense.

The designer was not long in conceiving the idea that was to be Russia's major contribution to the aerial combat of World War I. On an exhibition flight made in one of his earlier designs, Sikorsky had been forced down by engine failure—a frequent occurrence at the time—only to discover that the cause had been a mere mosquito that got trapped in the carburetor and cut off the fuel supply. If an engine could be disabled by something so minuscule, Sikorsky reasoned, then airplanes ought to have more than one engine. The result of that brainstorm was officially given the name *Russky Vityaz*—Russian Knight—but came to be known more simply and affectionately as the *Grand*.

The name was apt in every respect. The plane carried four 100-horsepower four-cylinder engines, which were mounted in a row on the leading edges of the lower wings. Those wings had a majestic span of 92 feet and were supported by 10 rows of struts and piano wire. The cabin was for the first time enclosed in glass, and the plane had dual controls and instruments to tell pilot and copilot how fast and how high they were flying—data that the pilot of any other plane of the day had to judge by the wind in his face and a talent known as "bird sense." At the rear of the

Towed by a team of school chums, aviation student Andrei N. Tupolev—later to become a renowned aircraft designer—takes off in a glider he constructed at the Moscow Higher Technical School in 1909. "In my second school year, I built my first glider," he recalled later. "In it I made my first flight, rising 10 to 15 meters."

cockpit a door led back to a separate cabin furnished with wicker chairs for the remaining crew members; besides pilot and copilot, this wondrous machine was intended to carry a navigator and a mechanic.

The plane had a disappointingly short life of only three months. It came to grief in a freak accident on the ground in August 1913. A small plane was flying over the field one day when suddenly its engine ripped off and hurtled down upon the *Grand*. The pilot of the offending plane skillfully glided his craft to landing without injury to himself, but the *Grand* was damaged beyond repair. Sikorsky had regarded the *Grand* as only an experiment anyway; he coolly ordered its usable parts salvaged and proceeded to build a bigger plane yet—the *Ilya Muromets*.

The I.M., as it came to be called, exceeded even the *Grand* in size and luxury. It had a wingspan of 102 feet and a length of more than 60 feet. And—mercifully for pilots who had to fly in the bitter Russian winters—it had interior heating, a luxury provided by two long steel tubes that brought in warmth generated by the engines.

Sikorsky proved that his craft was more than a mere curiosity; in July 1914 he made a historic flight from St. Petersburg to Kiev and back, a round trip of 1,600 miles, demonstrating that he had given the world a practical means of long-distance transport.

One month later, imperial Russia and the Allies joined in war against Germany. The Army had already placed an order for 10 I.M.s for use as bombers and now ordered another 32, and the Navy ordered one for itself. Together with the other craft built in Russia under license, and imports from the Allies and the United States, they enabled the Imperial Air Service to muster a frontline strength of 244 aircraft. That was far more than either France (with 138) or Great Britain (with 113) could claim. Only Germany came close, with 232 planes.

Scarcely anyone, either in Russia or elsewhere, had thought carefully about how to employ aircraft in war. The first and most obvious tasks

Beaming with pride, Tupolev (center, with hand on fuselage) stands beside his first powered aircraft, the ANT-1, which he built in 1921. With only a tiny 18-hp engine, the single-seat monoplane of wood and metal nonetheless managed to cruise at 62 mph and climb to 6,000 feet.

were the ones previously assigned to cavalry; scouting enemy positions and making hit-and-run raids on the enemy's rear. For reconnaissance missions planes could be equipped with cameras; and for raids they were provided with bombs to be hurled from aloft. But so casually did the belligerent nations approach air warfare in 1914 that their airmen flew unarmed, or armed only with pistols for hand-to-hand combat should an engine fail and force the fliers to land in enemy territory.

Naturally the arrival of enemy scouts aloft brought the urge to intercept them. But no tactics, no strategy and no precedents existed to guide the men who flew the new military vehicle. In their first encounters with enemy aircraft, airmen acted with impulsive bravado. The first recorded air battle was initiated by a Russian, Staff Captain Peter Nesterov, a 27-year-old squadron commander stationed in Galicia. Nesterov had won a certain celebrity—and a sharp reprimand—the year before, when he dared to put a Nieuport through a loop-the-loop, a then-untried maneuver of dives and climbs that, in the opinion of onlookers, could easily have torn the plane asunder in midair.

Now, in September 1914, when the War was scarcely five weeks old, three enemy planes appeared suddenly over the Galicia airfield. Flying in a tight V-formation, they bombed the hangars, the workshops and the aircraft parked on the field. As flames began to sweep through the hangars, Nesterov sprinted past the blaze, seized a Morane monoplane and took off to defy the enemy by the first means that came to mind— using the plane itself as a weapon. Climbing rapidly, he coolly pointed his craft at the leader of the German formation and smashed headlong into it. The other two planes departed; Nesterov's craft and his adversary's plunged to the ground, killing both pilots instantly. This time the Russian officials took a different view of their headstrong pilot; finding it salutary to exploit his bravery in the interests of boosting national morale, they buried him with full military honors in the tomb of an ancient Russian prince at Kiev and hailed him as a hero of Mother Russia.

In time, other Russian officers were to apply more thoughtful attention to aerial tactics. Staff Captain Alexander Kazakov, a former cavalry officer, hatched a notion that he could bring down enemy aircraft by means of an anchor suspended on a long steel cable from his machine. When he was posted to a frontline squadron, he had a Morane fitted with a winch and anchor, and on March 31, 1915, he took off, intending to claim his first victim—a German biplane observing artillery fire near the village of Guzov. Unfortunately Kazakov's anchor reel jammed as he began to unwind it, and he was unable to execute his novel idea. The enemy plane did not escape, however; in the emergency, Kazakov found another tactic. He climbed above the German plane, then calmly dived on its top wing and crumpled it with the Morane's undercarriage, sending the German plane hurtling to destruction. Kazakov crashlanded safely behind his own lines and lived to become the scourge of German pilots. In the next two years he was officially credited with 17 kills but probably accounted for twice that number of enemy aircraft.

French-designed Nieuports and Farmans are assembled in Moscow's Dux Works, a bicycle factory that in 1910 became Russia's biggest aircraft plant.

Like most fliers, Kazakov had entered aviation in a sporting spirit, and he abhorred the killing of fellow fliers. He always carried an icon of Saint Nicholas in the cockpit of his aircraft and invariably attended the funerals of pilots he sent down over Russian territory.

Meanwhile, designers everywhere were experimenting with ways to arm planes. At first they had mounted machine guns at an angle on the sides—which meant that the pilot had a difficult maneuver to perform before he could fire. It also meant that his craft was vulnerable fore and aft. Not until 1915, when the Frenchman Raymond Saulnier fitted a propeller with deflector plates that safeguarded the propeller blades, were planes able to fire straight ahead. Once Saulnier's mechanism was tested in action, the idea spread rapidly and was soon improved upon.

With that development, Russian Captain Yevgraf Kruten, a flamboyant flier who had his craft painted with the head of a medieval knight, devised several practical tactics for aerial combat. His favorite attack was to climb up under the unarmed tail of an enemy, then fire a short burst and dive rapidly away in a turn. Kruten was officially credited with seven German planes, but like Kazakov, he probably shot down many more. Kruten, too, was a chivalrous man. In June 1917, the body of one of his victims yielded a poignant memento, a charred photograph of the pilot with his wife and young child. Kruten promptly flew over the enemy lines and dropped a letter to the airman's widow, expressing regret that he had deprived the child of its father and the wife of her husband. Kruten himself was killed within the week—ironically, not in combat, but because he ran out of fuel and crashed while attempting to land.

Reconnaissance missions held less excitement than combat, but they constituted more than 90 per cent of all the sorties flown on the Eastern Front in World War I. And even reconnaissance pilots risked their lives; they were just as likely to be shot at, and the flier who came down in enemy territory had nothing but his wits and luck to save him. One Russian pilot told of a narrow escape after being shot down by ground fire on a mission over Poland. The flier, whom the records identify only by the tantalizingly cryptic abbreviation "Captain Tch-y," clambered out of his machine and sprinted for his life with German soldiers running right behind him—shooting, but not to kill; scouts were generally wanted alive for whatever information they might be induced to yield.

He had scant hope of escaping—until suddenly, over the top of a hill, he spied three Cossack horsemen galloping toward him. "I hardly know what happened next," he wrote, "but I found myself on horseback, clinging to the Cossack who had saved me and riding hard for home."

Aviation's other mission in war—bombing—was mainly done for Russia by Sikorsky's giant I.M.s, the biggest and widest-ranging planes in any of the world's air forces. The I.M.s almost failed to be included, however. When the great planes first arrived at the front at Bialystok, an important junction on the St. Petersburg-Warsaw rail line, they were not in the least welcome. Aside from the difficulty of flying the heavy craft,

Lieutenant Peter Nesterov stands beside his Nieuport monoplane at an air base near Kiev on September 9, 1913—the day that he became the first flier to loop the loop successfully. Twelve months later Nesterov sacrificed his life by deliberately ramming an enemy plane.

Aiming his unarmed Morane like a missile, Nesterov smashes into the foe in this commemorative plaque labeled "P. N. Nesterov's Ramming, 1914." The young pilot's spontaneous action inspired a desperate Soviet Air Force tactic in the early days of World War II.

air commanders found the planes to be a nightmare to maintain—particularly with the onset of the Russian winter in October. At least one I.M. lost its chassis taxiing over ground that had frozen into a corrugated grill. "The repairs will take three to five days," an officer telegraphed Army headquarters in mid-October. "I petition you if at all possible to send me two normal kind of planes." Complaints of that sort multiplied, and soon the order for additional I.M.s was canceled.

But Mikhail Shidlovsky, who had a vested interest in the pioneering craft, appealed to the Czar. The Czar intervened, the manufacture of I.M.s proceeded as planned and the Army's order was reinstated. However, to make sure that the planes would be properly used, the Czar commissioned Shidlovsky a major general in the Army and put him in command of a special Squadron of Flying Ships, composed solely of I.M.s. When Shidlovsky proceeded to the front, he took Sikorsky along to teach the men how to fly the planes and to oversee maintenance.

The two men arrived at the front in December 1914, and between them they had the squadron ready for its first raid in two months' time. On a crisp morning in February 1915, an Ilya Muromets lumbered across the lines at an altitude of 6,000 feet, dumped 600 pounds of bombs on German-held territory at Plotsk, a port city on the Vistula, and took photographs. The bombs did no damage to speak of, but the plane at last had gone into action and made a safe return. Nine days later the same I.M. bombed a German railway station in East Prussia, this time doing enough damage to prevent the movement of trains through the area; the plane returned 24 hours later and destroyed two ammunition trains that had been waiting to move since the previous day's raid. German gunners again tried but failed to shoot the I.M. down. Before long the members of the Flying Squadron had the pleasure of reading in a German newspaper that "the Russians have uncommon airplanes that do terrible damage and are not vulnerable to artillery."

One reason the great plane proved so hard to hit, at least in the beginning, was that its outsized dimensions made it seem closer than it was; German gunners who had never seen so large a craft in the sky misjudged their aim. Fighters that tried to tackle it had a different problem. "My aircraft was thrown back and forth by the strong prop wash of the giant," wrote one German pilot, "and I had to slow my aircraft down repeatedly to stabilize it and to keep from overtaking him."

That particular pilot had the rare experience of getting the better of an I.M. "I pushed full throttle and flew over the enemy aircraft in a sort of jump, and most of his fire passed below my aircraft," the German wrote. He then dropped closer to the I.M. so that his gunner could fire from a position slightly to the side of and above the cabin. He repeated this maneuver four times—and finally scored some hits. "I noticed the aircraft begin to wallow and then suddenly drop into a steep spiral. As the spin steepened, the outer part of the upper wing, on which the Russian insignia was painted, broke away and began to flutter down."

The I.M. plunged on until it crashed, and the German pilot brought his own plane to a safe landing. "We were greeted by a cheering group of soldiers who had observed the battle, which had lasted nearly 10 minutes," he wrote. "We left immediately to view the wreck of the giant aircraft, which had fallen about a mile and a quarter away." The Russian crew had not thought to drop their bombload before engaging in the fight; some of the bombs exploded when the plane crashed, blasting the I.M. to shards. "The basic structure of the aircraft could be recognized, but most of the smaller details had been destroyed in the crash," the German wrote. All four of the Russian crew were killed.

That I.M. was one of only two that were shot down in the entire course of the War. Even when hit, the plane displayed an incredible staying power. One I.M. returned from a raid riddled by no fewer than 374 shrapnel and bullet holes, and with a wing strut shot away; others returned with one or two engines out of commission.

I.M.s survived so many close calls that they inevitably inspired tales of derring-do by the men who flew them. One such tale told of a memorable raid in April 1916, when an Ilya Muromets attacked a railway station some distance behind enemy lines and flew into a barrage of anti-aircraft fire from German batteries dug in all around the station. With shrapnel ripping through the fabric-covered fuselage, the I.M. dropped its bombs from 8,000 feet, scoring several direct hits. When the last bombs were released and the pilot turned for home, he was hit in the chest by a shrapnel splinter. He slumped over the controls, his feet still on the pedals, and the great bomber stalled and went into a nose dive. Doom seemed certain—but the copilot scrambled forward in a trice. First he tried to drag the unconscious pilot out of the seat but was unable to budge the body; then he reached over the pilot and with a strength born of desperation managed to pull the craft out of its dive. Safely away from the antiaircraft fire, two other crewmen dragged the wounded pilot aft, and the copilot managed to get the I.M. back to base. When the plane finally rolled to a halt after landing, the right wing creaked ominously, drooped, then dropped clean away from the fuselage. It was later found that so many supporting stays had been damaged that only the air pressure exerted during flight had held the wing in place.

Over a period of two and a half years, Sikorsky made constant improvements on the plane. Among the most ingenious was a machine gun in the tail. A rear gun posed special problems, for the tail lay beyond a complex maze of supports too dense for a man to climb through rapidly when an enemy appeared. Sikorsky devised a sled that ran on rails along the floor of the fuselage. At a moment's notice the gunner could slide to the tail lying flat on his belly, unhindered by the maze of supports. "This installation proved to be extremely valuable and workable," Sikorsky wrote with pride. "After that time not one single I.M. was brought down, while more than 200 bombing raids were made."

Inevitably, the Army reversed its attitude toward the I.M.s. A staff officer on another front wired the Supreme High Command, asking: "Can't we have some planes like the Flying Squadron's I.M.s for use

Igor Sikorsky's "tramcar with wings"

The workers at St. Petersburg's Russo-Baltic Railcar Factory made fun of a gigantic four-engined aircraft they assembled in 1913, dubbing it "the tramcar with wings." But young Igor Sikorsky had a better name for his creation: He christened it the *Ilya Muromets*, after a mythical giant who rode a charger across the heavens.

Sikorsky's giant not only flew, it became a legend in its own right as the largest and most formidable bomber to see service in World War I. With four 220-hp engines and an enormous 102-foot wingspan, the I.M. could carry a bombload of three tons to a target nearly 250 miles away, then return.

Mastering the huge craft was no easy task. So heavy were the elevators that landing sometimes took the combined strength of the pilot and copilot pulling together on the control column—with the other five crew members sent aft to shift the center of gravity. Still, the I.M.s and their resourceful crews proved overwhelmingly successful, prompting one czarist general to exclaim: "Give me just three Murometses and take back all your light planes and I will be content!"

Fierce concentration etched on his face, Igor Sikorsky sits at the controls of his Ilya Muromets bomber, shortly before piloting the craft (above) on its maiden flight in 1913.

Russian soldiers load an Ilya Muromets with bombs before a mission in 1916. Early models had external bomb racks, but later ones had a bomb hatch in the fuselage floor.

Looking like an apartment corridor, the fuselage of an Ilya Muromets stretches back 30 feet to the tail. The I.M. was built of wood, braced with wire and covered with fabric. A flier's helmet hangs at left, just above and aft of some ballast sandbags stowed in an empty bomb rack.

The I.M. cockpit holds a pilot's seat, a bomb rack (right) and a bomb-sighting panel on the floor (left). The crosslines at bottom are cracks in the glass negative.

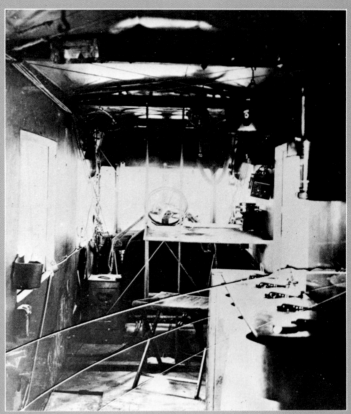

A gunner mans the two dorsal machine guns mounted atop the gas tanks in the break between the wings. In addition to their seven defensive guns, many I.M.s were equipped with armor plating on the cockpit floor and behind the pilots' seats.

An Ilya Muromets lies with a broken back, tail in the air, after an uncontrolled spin. The insignia of the Imperial Air Service appears on the fuselage and crumpled wings. Lateral instability made the I.M. a hard plane to fly, but only four of the 73 built were lost through crashes or enemy action in World War I.

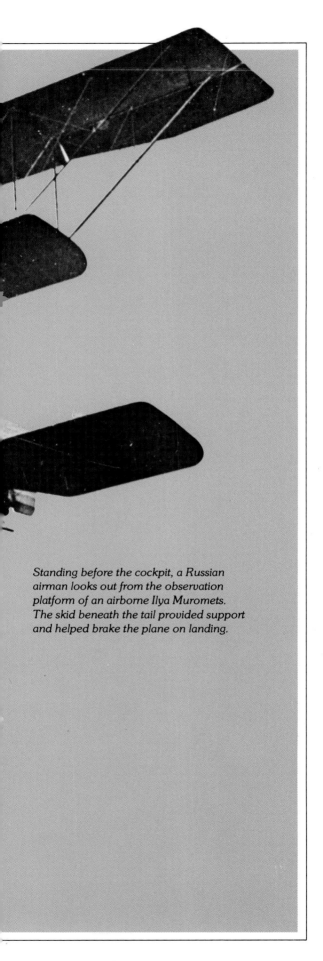

Standing before the cockpit, a Russian airman looks out from the observation platform of an airborne Ilya Muromets. The skid beneath the tail provided support and helped brake the plane on landing.

here?" But the Supreme High Command could not oblige, for there were not enough I.M.s to go around.

Though the I.M.s earned most of the plaudits, they constituted only a tiny fraction of the swiftly growing Imperial Air Service. Spurred on by the War, the production of aircraft was soaring; by 1917 the number of aircraft factories had more than doubled to 18, and the annual output of planes had risen from approximately 400 to about 2,200. Here and there a few Russian designers, in addition to Sikorsky, were beginning to try their wings. One young aeronautical engineer, Dmitri Grigorovich, made some promising designs for flying boats—pontoon-fitted craft for use by the Navy in the Baltic and Black Seas. An American pilot who inspected Grigorovich's single-engined M-9s on maneuvers saw seven of the planes lowered from naval vessels and launched into the air in 15 minutes. Unlike the British, who folded the wings of their seaplanes and stored the craft in shipboard hangars, the Russians kept the M-9s on deck and hoisted them off directly, losing no time in assembling and maneuvering them into place.

M-9s generally sought out enemy shipping as targets, but half a dozen M-9s took part in strategic bombing against the enemy's home front—a novel action in 1917. They dropped some 50 bombs on Lake Terko Dam, source of the water supply of Constantinople. The bombs hit their target, and the pilots reported considerable damage—though there is no record of any serious effect on life in the Turkish capital.

Grigorovich was to provide Russia with excellent aircraft in the future, as was another designer, a young genius by the name of Nikolai Polikarpov, who was taken on at the Russo-Baltic Railcar Factory and put in charge of I.M. production. For the nonce, however, Polikarpov was limited to carrying out Sikorsky's designs.

What few other planes originated in Russian factories had little to recommend them. One small reconnaissance biplane, built in Odessa, was approved for production despite the terrifying fact that in flight its lateral control and stability were virtually nonexistent. When it arrived at the front it inflicted far more casualties among Russian pilots than on the enemy. Another scout plane, the Lebed XII, named for the designer and factory owner V. A. Lebedev, was so badly laid out that exhaust fumes from the engine nearly asphyxiated the pilot and his observer. Both aircraft were withdrawn from service after a few months.

The foreign planes made under license were not much better. French-designed Nieuport scouts built in Russia displayed an alarming tendency to dive without warning; after a number of accidents it was discovered that the wings were being fitted at the wrong angle. And practically all Russian-built planes compared unfavorably with their German rivals in speed, rate of climb, ceiling and range. In most cases the defects could be ascribed to inadequate training of the factory workers, a result of Russia's tardy entrance into the industrial world.

Planes continued to be imported—France, Britain and the U.S. together provided about 900 aircraft to Russia between 1914 and

Three Ilya Muromets bombers are housed in tent hangars at the Yablonna airfield in Poland, home of the czarist Flying Ship Squadron of World War I. At lower right, one of the bombers has been rolled out of its tent by the ground crew.

An Ilya Muromets bomber, its wing sections loaded on horse-drawn wagons, is delivered to the front in 1914. The factory that produced the huge aircraft lacked an airfield; hence the plane was shipped overland as a kit and assembled at its destination.

1917—but the Allies had their own priorities. The French had lost so heavily at Verdun in 1916 that they subsequently curtailed shipments of Nieuport fighters. Russian fliers on the Eastern Front complained that, instead of the latest French machines they had been promised, they were given roughly patched-up rejects from the Western Front.

To make matters worse, maintenance was a constant problem for the Russians. First of all, maintenance crews were no more skilled than factory workers. Secondly, the plethora of foreign designs meant that spare engines and other parts could not be used interchangeably. Spares of any kind were forever in short supply at the front because on top of everything else Russia's roads and railways were inadequate to deal with the War's massive movements of troops and matériel. All those sorry facts combined to inflict a severe rate of attrition; few aircraft exceeded 80 hours' operational flight. With a growing lack of confidence in their machines and a soaring casualty list, Russian fliers at the front inevitably suffered a disastrous drop in morale.

What they heard about conditions at home did nothing to raise their spirits. Food was short, workers were staging protest demonstrations, revolutionary groups were circulating seditious literature, and the Czar was being charged with dereliction in the conduct of the War. By July 1917 peasants were plundering their landlords' estates; workers were looting factories and taking control from the owners.

The turning point came on the evening of November 7, 1917, when a cadre of political revolutionaries known as Bolsheviks and led by the fiery orator Vladimir Ilyich Lenin seized the government. Lenin lost no time in demonstrating his concern about the air force. Within three days

of assuming power he appointed eight commissars to an aviation board, and within weeks he announced his intention to "preserve intact all air units and flying schools for the working people." As part of a careful campaign to rid the air force of all association with the fallen Czar and to engage popular sentiment, the leaders named the new force the Workers' and Peasants' Red Air Fleet.

The Bolsheviks inherited from the czarist regime an air force with a strength of approximately 1,000 machines and an aircraft industry with a force of about 10,000 laborers capable of turning out upward of 2,000 aircraft annually. But terrible struggles lay ahead. The Bolsheviks had to fight to hold their power; and between some bad luck on the battlefields and inexperience on their own account, they squandered so much of the air force that within three years there was virtually nothing left.

On the war front, the effect of the Bolshevik coup was to bring an utter breakdown of military discipline. Nowhere was the chaos worse than in the Imperial Air Service. At airfields along the front, work came to a standstill; aircraft were abandoned where they stood. Ground crews of one squadron tried to fly home in the unit's fighters; they only succeeded in wrecking the planes. Others mutinied, setting up "soldiers' committees" to take over control from the officers.

Most officers were either aristocrats or at least upper-class representatives of the old imperial regime, and hundreds were shot out of hand. Among the casualties was General Shidlovsky, who had enabled Sikorsky to build the pioneering I.M.s and who as an army commander had led the celebrated Squadron of Flying Ships. Hundreds of officers escaped to the West or went underground to join anti-Bolshevik groups.

Only about a third of all the pilots in the Imperial Air Service continued to fly for the Bolsheviks. And those who did posed a nagging threat to the Bolshevik leaders, who lived constantly in dread of a counter-revolution. The Bolsheviks therefore put all former czarist officers under close observation by political commissars to ensure that they displayed no antirevolutionary tendencies. The commissars exercised the real power in the air force; no order was valid unless it was countersigned by a commissar, and no planes flew without a commissar's approval.

To overcome the shortage of pilots, the leaders rounded up young Bolsheviks who could be counted on to be of "proletarian origin and committed to the Revolution" and brusquely ordered them to learn to fly in whatever aircraft were available. Not all recruits were keen on flying, and many were not even fit to fly. Alexei Tumansky, an ex-czarist pilot who went over to the Reds, found out just how little enthusiasm some of his new fellow pilots had when he interviewed a young trainee who came to Tumansky's squadron fresh from Moscow Flying School.

"Have you done any bombing?" Tumansky asked the youth.

"Once, with an instructor. He did the bombing and I watched," the youth replied.

"Do you know anything about machine guns?"

"We didn't have to do any air gunnery."

"How much time have you spent in the air?"

"Well, not a lot. I guess about 40 hours."

"How did you enter the air force? Volunteer or conscript?"

"Conscript! Wild horses wouldn't have got me into the air."

At the other extreme were daredevils who proved to be more of a hazard than a help. One Red flier, Georgi Sapozhnikov, was due to give a flying display in a French Spad that he had rakishly decorated with a black ace of spades on the fuselage, a black arrow on the tail and black stars on the wings. Unfortunately, Sapozhnikov had celebrated too much the night before, and was in no condition to fly on the morning of the air show. His mechanic, hoping to avert disaster, disconnected the ignition switch. But Sapozhnikov, not to be fooled, drew a pistol and made the mechanic fix the switch. He then climbed unsteadily into the Spad, revved up and took off at full speed, pulling into a steep climb the moment he left the ground. At this critical point the engine failed. For a split second, the Spad seemed to hang in the air; then it plunged to the ground and crashed in a ball of fire. No one knows how many airmen destroyed both themselves and their craft by such suicidal bravado.

The aircraft industry was in no condition to replace any losses. In the chaos of the Revolution, workers fled to the countryside with their families in search of farmland and food. Even more damaging to the industry were the punitive measures taken by the authorities against some of Russia's outstanding scientists, designers and engineers, who, like the officers, were anathema among the revolutionaries; many were murdered, imprisoned or otherwise made to disappear. Among those who escaped was Igor Sikorsky; he made his way to Murmansk, boarded a steamer and sailed for the West. In March 1919 he landed in New York, where a long and distinguished career lay ahead of him.

In that terrible state—lacking officers, pilots, matériel, designers and an industry to support them—the Bolsheviks still had to face the exigencies of war. Early in 1918, Germany launched a massive offensive and swept over Russian positions in Estonia, Latvia and the Ukraine, capturing more than 500 Russian aircraft that had been left standing unguarded on their airfields. One czarist convert to the Reds, Colonel Joseph Bashko, managed to fly his crew and his pet bulldog to safety in an I.M. before the Germans arrived. But there were not enough fliers to save all the big bombers, and elsewhere along the front Russian men burned 30 of them to prevent their falling into German hands.

The Reds were still reeling from the terrible loss of aircraft when civil war broke out in the spring of 1918. The Workers' and Peasants' Air Fleet was committed to defend the Revolution with odd detachments of aircraft scattered over the vastness of Russia—and only a handful of pilots to fly them. Trouble flared when anti-Bolshevik groups and former Imperial Army officers, loosely grouped as the "White" forces, seized control of territory that stretched east across Siberia from the Volga River to the Pacific Ocean. Uprisings occurred in the north, the west and the south as one group after another contested the Bolsheviks' right to rule. Meanwhile, the Western powers signed an armistice in November 1918, bringing World War I to a close. From the Red standpoint a major effect of the Armistice was to bring in legions of the old Russian Empire's allies on the side of the Whites. In the bitter, confused fighting that followed for the next two years, the Reds were engaged at various times against the forces of some 20 different governments and nationalist groups, in actions that spread across Eastern Europe.

The Red fliers met their severest test in the south, where ex-Imperial Army General Peter Wrangel undertook a series of major offensives aimed at Moscow. A prime objective was Tsaritsyn, an old city on the Volga whose name reflected association with generations of Czars, or Tsars, as the word was sometimes spelled. The defenses of the city were for a time in the charge of one of Lenin's most ambitious lieutenants; his name was Joseph Stalin, and in later years, when he took imperial prerogatives unto himself, he would bestow his own name on this coveted city and call it Stalingrad.

The Whites' attack on the city was supported by two Royal Air Force squadrons that were equipped with British Camels and D.H.9s and commanded by World War I aces with many kills to their credit.

In the spring of 1919, as the Whites advanced on Tsaritsyn, the Red Air Fleet met the seasoned RAF for the first time. Four RAF Camels went on a scouting mission north of the town, and a flight of Red Nieuport 28s undertook to stop them. In the dogfight that followed, the Reds were no match for the crack British fliers, and one of the Red Nieuports was shot

Fledgling fliers for the Czar

In 1910, when the Imperial War Ministry established the Gatchina Aviation School near St. Petersburg, only a few visionaries believed in the military value of aircraft. Many of the converts were cavalrymen, whose mission had long been reconnaissance and whose views were aptly put by one young officer: "On the battlefield, a dwarf who can see will conquer a blind giant." Indeed, cavalrymen were among the first to apply for the initial class of 30 students at Gatchina.

Cadets were housed in a nobleman's unused summer palace on a vast estate of fallow wheat fields. The planes were of French design, and a cadre of French mechanics and instructors went along to train Russian counterparts.

The school's objective was to turn out full-fledged aeronautical experts, proficient in theory, design and maintenance as well as flight and navigation; when not in the air or at ground school, cadets were required to help out as line mechanics and fabric riggers.

Flying instruction began with a series of taxiing runs to familiarize the student with aileron and rudder controls. Cadets then went up as passengers; from a separate cockpit behind the pilot, the student would lean forward and rest his hand atop the instructor's to learn control-stick coordination. After several such flights, he might solo, and after approximately 100 hours of flying time, he would graduate—if he survived.

The Farman 4 primary trainer was a biplane of especially evil disposition. The 50-hp engine lacked a throttle, so all maneuvers, including landings, were performed at full power—which was probably just as well since the Farman stalled at anything less than top speed. Even then, the plane would accept only the shallowest of turns; otherwise it would spin to earth. Equally unnerving, a broad belt of high trees traversed the landing area, and it snared many an unwary student; the cadets asked to have the trees cut down, but the nobleman refused.

The Russians persevered nonetheless, and in the next few years, the trickle of pilots graduating from Gatchina became a stream. By 1914, when Russia entered World War I, Gatchina and a smaller school at Sevastopol had trained 300 pilots and were pinning wings on 130 new fliers a year. And this at a time when in all the United States, cradle of aviation, there were scarcely 25 qualified pilots.

At the Gatchina Aviation School, a group of cadets wheels a newly assembled Farman 4 trainer out of its hangar, at left.

Four Nieuport monoplanes with skis, used for advanced instruction, await takeoff in 1913.

Careful to remain near the ground, a novice flier makes his first solo flight in a Farman 4 in 1916.

A crumpled Farman 22 biplane offers Gatchina cadets an object lesson in the difficulties of landing such a fragile aircraft.

Put together from the remains of a crashed plane, this odd-looking contraption served Gatchina as a fire truck and ambulance.

down. Undeterred, two Red fighters rose the next day to intercept a formation of D.H.9 bombers that had attacked the Bolshevik headquarters in Tsaritsyn, but they were beaten off by fighter escorts.

Later in the week, a spectacular dogfight took place over the Volga, where a string of Soviet barges was heading downriver with a shipment of aircraft bound for Red headquarters. RAF bombers, escorted by half a dozen RAF Camels, began to bomb the barges, and half a dozen Red Spads and Nieuports raced aloft to fight them off. Two Red planes spiraled out of the battle and crashed in flames, but this time two Camels were badly damaged before the engagement was broken off. Nothing had been decided—but the Soviet pilots had shown new fighting skill.

For the inexperienced officers that the Reds put in command, combat flying could be a terrifying experience. The veteran Alexei Tumansky left an account of just how troublesome it could be to have a neophyte on board. "We saw our target, the armored train, from a distance," Tumansky wrote, and "went straight into the attack." Raining bombs down on the train, he made three runs and saw that he had caused some damage; the rear car of the train was canted over on its side. "I still had about ten 20-pound bombs left and I started to descend in order to get in close and make my remaining bombs tell," Tumansky went on. "Then all at once, my commanding officer appeared beside me, seized hold of the control stick, and pointing to a large hole in the port wing, shouted for me to turn for home. Competing with the thunder of bursting shells, I tried to reassure him that there was nothing to worry about and that I would soon finish off the train—but he refused to let go the stick and kept on shouting 'Home!' and I dared not pry his hands off."

In June 1919, the Reds got their bitterest taste yet of enemy air power. At this point, Wrangel's White army was at the gates of Tsaritsyn, and the Reds were grimly holding on to the city with a handful of men. Wrangel learned that a Red relief column was heading toward the town with 3,000 cavalry. He ordered one of the British squadrons to attack the Red horsemen as they threaded their way through the gullies and ravines north of the town. The RAF planes proved murderous, diving again and again onto the column, strafing men and horses with merciless machine-gun fire. In the narrow confinement of the pass, the Red soldiers had nowhere to escape or find shelter. They were mowed down where they stood, and by the time the last White fighter had disappeared, the pass was choked with the dead and dying. The Reds withdrew their troops from Tsaritsyn just in the nick of time and left the city temporarily to the Whites. They had learned a brutal lesson: The frightful aerial bombardment of their land forces would remain forever seared in memory.

The Whites did not hold Tsaritsyn long; in October the Reds mounted a massive counterattack. The Reds now had one advantage, and they exploited it well: With resistance knocked out in the north, the east and the west, they gathered up aircraft from all those regions and focused their strength in this one area—setting a precedent for such concentra-

In the center of their squadron's ammunition dump, Soviet ground crewmen arm bombs on the Turkestan Front during the Civil War in 1920. The

weapons include a machine gun (right), small incendiary bombs (center) and fragmentation bombs (far right). The planes are British-built Sopwiths.

With its "pilot" riding in the cockpit, a truck-mounted airplane parades through a Soviet town in 1923 during a grass-roots campaign to publicize and raise money for the Red Air Force. The exhibit was sponsored by the Society of Friends of the Air Fleet, one of many air-minded civilian organizations throughout the country.

tions of power as the one they would later amass at Kursk. At Tsaritsyn they mustered nearly 40 aircraft. It was the greatest Red air fleet yet to be thrown into a single battle anywhere.

Among the planes sent south for the drive were two I.M.s that survived from World War I. The huge four-engined craft were particular favorites of the Red fliers, who coveted the chance to pilot them. There was one drawback to flying the I.M.s, and that was no fault of the planes'. Red commanders, eager to pack them with ever bigger bombloads, sometimes skimped on fuel to save weight. Alexei Tumansky recalled being once forced down for want of fuel about six or seven miles from his base. The only place to land was in a bog, and even if fuel had been fetched, the plane would not have been able to take off again from the marshy ground. The only solution was to dismantle the craft and then lug all five tons of it, part by part, to the airfield.

The heavy loading with bombs had another effect, and that was to limit the planes to an altitude of 2,600 feet or less. The low altitude was in one respect an advantage, for it gave the bombardiers better aim on their targets—and struck terror into the hearts of their adversaries, as Tumansky found out when flying an I.M. on a mission against a White military train and supply dump in central Belorussia. He had been told that the target was heavily protected by antiaircraft batteries, and indeed as he approached the guns began to fire. Then, to his surprise and delight, the batteries fell silent as the gunners deserted their posts one after another. Tumansky was able to circle the base three times, allowing his crew plenty of time to drop the bombs. The I.M.s were so outsized and their bombloads so massive that their mere appearance overhead was often enough to create panic on the ground.

Out of the frightful memories of Tsaritsyn, where their own cavalry had been at the mercy of strafing by White bombers, and out of the practical necessity of flying the heavy I.M.s so low, a Soviet specialty was born. Could designers develop a particular plane for low-flying assaults? Lenin wanted to know. Not yet, but among the mechanics who traveled with the air force maintenance crews was a youth named Sergei Ilyushin. For the present he was confined to the tedious work of patching up damaged aircraft so they could fly again. But within two decades he was to design the fateful Il-2s, the Shturmoviks of World War II.

No one could say the novice Red Air Fleet won the Civil War for the Bolsheviks. But almost everywhere that fighting occurred, Red airmen went aloft to assist. And the Reds turned back White thrusts one by one until by November 1920 they had driven the last remnants of Wrangel's White army into the Crimea and to the edge of the sea at Sevastopol. All along the way, Red aircraft tore into the White cavalry columns, and harassed White troop formations, armored trains, rail junctions, supply depots and airfields. When at last the Whites abandoned Sevastopol on November 21, 1920, the Civil War was over.

Six years of war and revolution had exacted a terrible toll on the air force. Of the 1,000 or so planes the Reds had inherited from the Czar, only about 300 remained, and many of those were either unserviceable or obsolete. Moreover, new aircraft were not being produced in sufficient numbers to make good the losses sustained in action, since the Russian aviation industry remained in a shambles. Factories had managed to produce fewer than 700 planes during the Civil War. The work force of 10,000 had dwindled to less than 3,500.

To get the industry back on its feet, Lenin called for a mobilization of aircraft workers, placing them in the same category as soldiers on active duty and making them subject to the same discipline. All wood and metal workers, engineers and technicians between the ages of 17 and 50 who had worked in the aircraft industry for six months or more during the past decade were ordered to help rebuild the Red Air Fleet.

To pay for this, Lenin allocated 35 million gold rubles from a cache seized from the Czar's Treasury; some of the money was to be spent to revive the Soviet aircraft industry and some to buy planes abroad.

But Soviet purchasing agents were unwelcome in France, Britain and the U.S. During the Civil War the Reds had earned the enmity of Russia's former partners. The Reds found a solution in one of the oddest, most clandestine bargains ever struck between two nations. In April 1922 they signed a secret pact with their erstwhile foes, the Germans, who were forbidden by the Versailles Treaty to maintain an air force, build military aircraft or train pilots. Six months later, unbeknownst to the Western Allies, 400 German engineers and technicians arrived at Fili, a suburb of Moscow, to build a modern aircraft factory with designs and equipment provided by Hugo Junkers, one of the most innovative of German designers. At Fili the Soviets' best engineers could absorb advanced technology, with German instructors providing the tutelage and Russian laborers providing the sinew. The plans called for an annual production of 300 planes, some for the Red Air Fleet and others to be used at a flying school at Lipetsk, 250 miles southeast of Moscow, where a German staff taught Russian and German students.

By the beginning of 1925, some 60 German officers and 100 German technicians were transmitting to a new generation of Russian and German pilots the latest techniques of military flying—and at a safe remove from the prying eyes of the Allied commissioners who kept watch on Germany. No detail was spared to keep the arrangement secret; the German trainees wore Red Air Fleet uniforms and answered to Russian names. After a four- or five-month tour of duty they returned to peaceable occupations in their homeland—only to reemerge years later as the cadre of the Luftwaffe. And though the arrangement persisted for nearly a decade, it remained a secret until after World War II.

Meanwhile, Leon Trotsky, who was Lenin's War Commissar and the Bolshevik Party's most articulate spokesman, had taken measures to ensure that, as it grew, the Red Air Fleet should receive the all-important backing of the people. On March 6, 1923, using the newspaper *Pravda* as his platform, he published a long editorial under the headline "The Air Fleet: The Order of the Day." In it he announced the birth of a new Society of Friends of the Air Fleet, an organization designed to stimulate "air-mindedness" throughout the population.

The Russian people joined the society in droves. At the end of a year it boasted a membership of one million, and in three years more that figure would nearly double. The society published a monthly magazine, *Samolyot (Airplane),* sponsored flying displays, lectures and exhibitions, and taught schoolchildren how to build model airplanes. Members or not, visitors to the first All-Russian Agricultural Show in Moscow in 1923 could take joy rides in a Junkers F 13, an all-metal monoplane. Within a decade, society members were learning to fly for themselves at 21 aviation schools operating more than 100 airfields, where Red Air Force personnel served as instructors.

The society spared no effort to engage the sentiments of the workers and to link aviation with patriotism. Soviet aircraft factories were hung with banners exhorting the workers to ever greater efforts with such slogans as WORKERS! BUILD AN AIR FLEET! and PROLETARIAT! TAKE TO THE AIR! In exchange for a day's pay, workers could have the privilege of seeing an aircraft named after their factory or trade union or after some popular hero of their choosing, such as Lenin. That forceful man had meanwhile suffered a series of strokes, and when he died in January 1924 he was succeeded by Joseph Stalin, who had become the most powerful figure of the Bolshevik—now Communist—Party. As head of the nation, he was also to be the driving force behind the Red Air Force.

Just how vital an air force was to Stalin and his government would be manifest before the end of the decade. "One of the important achievements of the past five years has been the creation of the Red Air Force," asserted the Central Committee, which Stalin dominated, in 1929. "Our most important task of the next few years must be to catch up with the leading bourgeois countries in the matter of quality and to direct all effort toward creating, promoting and developing our own Soviet cadres of scientists, designers and engineers."

At a 1923 air show outside Moscow, Russian civilians relax on the airfield fringe or roam among a squadron's fighter planes.

Gigantic symbols of Soviet technology

When the gigantic, eight-engined *Maxim Gorky* made its debut over Moscow on June 19, 1934, Soviet citizens everywhere felt a surge of pride. To talk about the *Gorky* was to speak in superlatives. With its 206-foot wingspan and fantastic 117,000-pound takeoff weight, it was by far the largest aircraft in the world. Its 162-mph speed exceeded that of many fighter planes, and its 1,250-mile range enabled it to fly from Moscow to Leningrad and return without refueling.

The war-making potential of the *Maxim Gorky* was not lost on the Soviet Union's neighbors in the mid-1930s. The nation that produced such an awesome aircraft could—and did—build great fleets of long-range heavy bombers. But this particular symbol of Soviet technology, of Communist power and progress, was intended to carry not bombs but propaganda. Designed by Andrei Tupolev, foremost among Soviet aircraft builders, and named in honor of a contemporary Russian writer, the plane was fitted out to be the flagship of a unique propaganda squadron whose mission was to spread the government's messages to the most remote corners of a vast nation.

The *Gorky,* or ANT-20 as it was formally designated, was superbly equipped for the task. Enormous flaps and powerful brakes on the wheels enabled the plane to land at 62 mph on quarter-mile dirt strips, where crowds gathered under the wings to gawk and to be propagandized. If landing was impractical, the *Gorky* provided a spectacular flyover, showering pamphlets, booming out loudspeaker music and messages, flashing huge images on overhead clouds and forming patriotic slogans with a bank of red light bulbs on the underside of the wings.

Although the *Maxim Gorky* came to a calamitous end in 1935, after a midair collision with one of its fighter escorts, it was replaced a few years later by another giant, designated as the ANT-20bis. Virtually identical to the *Gorky,* except that it mounted six, more powerful engines instead of the original eight, the ANT-20bis was fitted out as a long-range airliner that could carry 64 passengers and a crew of eight. Eventually 16 were built, and many were still in service at the end of World War II.

Escorted by two gnatlike I-4 fighters, the Maxim Gorky flies over Moscow's Red Square during a 1935 military parade.

At a factory near Moscow, workers cover a Gorky wing with sheets of corrugated aluminum alloy. On the wing is a flight engineer's station.

The Gorky sits on the factory airfield after roll-out. Its huge wings, which covered 5,230 square feet, could lift 25 tons to an altitude of 19,000 feet.

A Gorky-like ANT-20bis, with sleeping compartments built into its thick wing roots, loads passengers for a long-distance flight.

An airborne propaganda mill

The *Maxim Gorky* was supplied with everything conceivable for its propaganda missions: a printing press, a photographic laboratory, a radio room, a dining room that could be quickly converted into a compact movie theater, and sleeping quarters for the use of the dozen government information specialists who lived and worked aboard the mammoth aircraft. The eight-member flight crew included three engineers, two of them stationed in wing blisters from which they could observe the performance of the 12-cylinder, 900-hp engines. If necessary, the engineers could service the wing engines in flight from passageways with five to seven feet of headroom.

1 RADIO RECEIVERS
2 GALLEY
3 MOVIE PROJECTION ROOM
4 DINING AREA
5 BAGGAGE COMPARTMENT
6 SLEEPING QUARTERS
7 FUEL TANKS
8 PHOTOGRAPHIC LABORATORY
9 WING PASSAGEWAYS
10 CLOAKROOMS
11 ELECTRICAL ROOM
12 WRITERS' COMPARTMENTS
13 TELEPHONE SWITCHBOARD
14 RADIO TRANSMITTERS
15 PASSENGER CABIN
16 PILOT'S COMPARTMENT
17 NAVIGATOR'S COMPARTMENT
18 LAVATORY
19 PRINTING PRESS
20 MECHANIC'S OBSERVATION POST

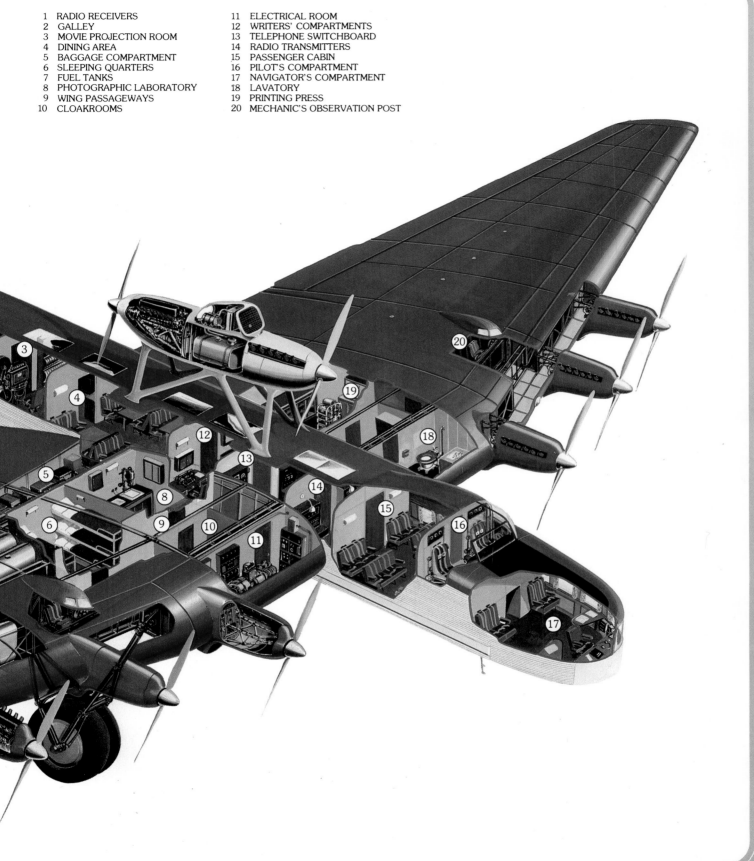

Mother hens with deadly chicks

By 1935, the Soviet Union possessed more long-range heavy bombers than all the other world powers combined—almost 1,000 giant warplanes, including 800 four-engined Tupolev TB-3s *(right),* which could lumber 800 miles nonstop with a 6,000-pound bombload. Yet for all their imposing weaponry, Soviet Air Force tacticians had long worried about the vulnerability of their bomber fleets in time of war. Flying deep into enemy territory, even the biggest bombers might be overwhelmed by swarms of hostile interceptors unless they could be protected by long-range fighter escorts. A possible solution came from an imaginative young engineer named Vladimir Vakhmistrov, who had the idea of converting some of the big bombers into airborne aircraft carriers that could launch conventional short-range fighters.

In the mid-1930s, Vakhmistrov began a remarkable series of experiments using various combinations of bombers, known as "mother hens," and fighters, called "chicks" or "parasites." He worked his way up to an incredible finale in 1935: a TB-3 carrying and launching no fewer than five escort fighters.

Interest in parasites waned in the late 1930s, partly because of technical problems and partly because Soviet doctrine shifted away from long-range bombardment in favor of close ground support. But Vakhmistrov's work was not totally in vain. During World War II, a unit of six TB-3s, each carrying a brace of I-16 fighter-bombers, operated out of the Crimea until late 1942, successfully attacking targets in Rumania and the Ukraine.

A formation of the Far East Command's TB-3 heavy bombers patrols the Amur River border between the Soviet Union and China in 1936. A transport version of the TB-3 could carry three tons of freight or 30 fully equipped paratroopers.

An I-4 fighter is rolled up a wooden ramp onto the wing of a twin-engined TB-1 bomber in 1931 before one of the first attempts at launching parasite fighters from an airborne carrier. The initial tests were successful, to the chagrin of skeptical military observers, who had belittled what they called "Vakhmistrov's circus."

Three I-5 fighters are securely clamped to the wings and fuselage of a TB-3 bomber in a 1932 variation of the experiment. Although all three of the fighters were launched without mishap, this arrangement was discarded because of the difficulty involved in mounting the center plane.

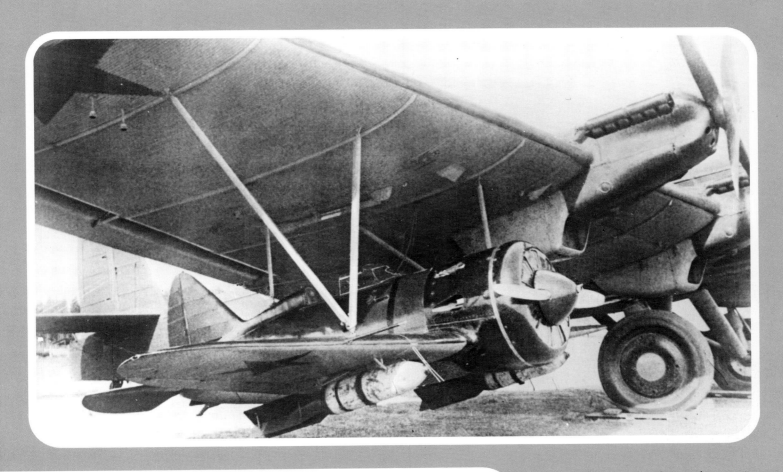

An I-16 fighter-bomber, packing a pair of 500-pound bombs, rests under the wing of its TB-3 mother plane during World War II. The big plane could ferry a pair of these speedy craft hundreds of miles into enemy territory, where they would dive-bomb small but important targets—often bridges—and still have enough fuel to get back to a Soviet air base.

One of the first launches of manned fighters from a plane in flight is captured in this historic 1931 photograph. The engines of all three aircraft were used to lift the contraption to 10,000 feet, where two sets of restraining clamps were released.

Six aircraft fly as one in this 1935 demonstration, which was popularly known as "Vakhmistrov's bouquet." The TB-3 took off with two I-5s above the wings and a pair of I-16s below. At 3,000 feet, a retractable trapeze was lowered, permitting an airborne I-Z fighter to hook on before all five of the planes were released.

In this 1934 demonstration, a highly maneuverable I-Z fighter, equipped with a hook, catches the bottom rung of a 13-foot-long trapeze fitted to a TB-3. The fighter could then be released or lifted up against the fuselage, where it could land safely with its mother plane.

2

Waging peace, testing for war

The prototype fighter plane that emerged from State Aircraft Factory No. 39 one morning in 1930 bore a curious designation on its fuselage: the letters *VT* boldly inscribed inside a red star. The red star was of course familiar as the symbol of the Bolshevik Revolution. But the *VT* stood for *Vnutrennaya Tyur'ma,* literally "internal prison," and indicated that the fighter had been built under strange circumstances indeed.

Located near Moscow, State Aircraft Factory No. 39 was in fact a Soviet penitentiary. Not only was the plane the product of convict labor, even more remarkable, the two inmates who designed it were among the nation's most talented aeronautical engineers. One was Dmitri Grigorovich, creator of the flying boats that had served the Czar's Navy in World War I. The other was Nikolai Polikarpov, who had succeeded Igor Sikorsky in overseeing production of Ilya Muromets bombers at the Russo-Baltic Railcar Factory; since then Polikarpov had designed several highly successful craft, among them the ubiquitous PO-2 biplane *(pages 94-95).* But in 1927 dictator Joseph Stalin had demanded a superior Russian-designed, Russian-built fighter for the Air Force—and when two years had passed and neither Grigorovich nor Polikarpov had produced a serviceable fighter, both designers were clapped into prison and ordered to create under the unrelenting eye of the state.

The anomaly of expecting genius to flourish in prison was something that could have happened only in the Russia of the 1920s and 1930s. Yet nothing better reflects the urgency with which Soviet leaders viewed the need for a large, modern air force—or the mood and methods of Stalin, who was shaping the colossal new state in his own fierce image.

The instrument for effecting Stalin's will was the secret police, known as the NKVD. The secret police kept a close watch on Soviet citizens in every walk of life; those associated with aviation encountered its omnipresence in research, production, performance aloft, strategy and tactics in battle. Any mistake by a designer, an engineer, a factory manager or a military officer might lead to a summons to the NKVD's grim chambers—or worse, arrest on the spot and a journey to headquarters

Soviet dictator Joseph Stalin confers with Marshal Semyon Budenny (center) and Air Force chief Yakov Alksnis in 1936 during the Red Air Force's build-up. Alksnis was later executed in the Great Purge.

in the black wagons known as "ravens." The number of arrests and imprisonments mounted until, by the latter part of the 1930s, the secret police was engaged in a monumental purge; then arrest and imprisonment gave way to mass murder on an unprecedented scale.

Under the lash or no, Soviet aviation made great strides throughout the decade. By the mid-1930s, the industry employed 350,000 workers, who labored in three shifts around the clock. "The impression is that with 10 times as many personnel employed as the French, the Soviet industry is producing 20 times as many aircraft," wrote Louis Charles Breguet, a French aircraft maker who toured the Soviet Union in 1936. With their new, and by now all-Russian, planes the Soviets avidly competed for every record in the skies—and claimed no fewer than 62 world marks for speed, altitude and distance by 1938.

Nevertheless, for all their numbers and much-publicized peacetime triumphs, Soviet planes and Soviet fliers often proved unexpectedly weak when called upon to fight: in the Spanish Civil War, where they were no match for the nascent German Luftwaffe; in Manchuria, where they at first struggled against an inferior Japanese air force; in Finland, where, certain of immediate victory, they were grievously embarrassed by a minuscule band of doughty fliers in obsolete craft. All the while, the Soviets inexplicably failed to prepare for—or even apparently perceive—the growing menace of Nazi Germany, which by decade's end was flying unfriendly reconnaissance missions over Russian soil.

The end product of this bewildering mixture of successes and failures, of keen perception and abysmal blindness, was the air force with which the Soviets entered World War II in 1941. The story can be said to have begun with the demands on Polikarpov and Grigorovich to build a proper fighter plane.

As early as 1925, Soviet leaders had decreed that Russia must have fighters of native design and manufacture and that all foreign aircraft were to be removed from frontline service "without delay." The demand was unrealistic, for the Soviet Air Force was still totally dependent on foreign designs—British de Havillands, German Heinkels and Junkers, Italian Ansaldos and Savoias. And 80 per cent of those were reconnaissance planes; the Red Air Force had few fighters of any kind. Moreover, Soviet engineers could ill afford to spurn foreign expertise; their nation was still so industrially backward that workmen had to cut every length of supporting wire and shape every propeller blade by hand. But the memory of having been hamstrung for want of foreign planes in World War I was all too raw, and in 1928 Stalin launched the first of several five-year plans that aimed to make Russia industrially self-sufficient. The plan called for an air arm that would surpass in size the forces of all neighboring potential enemies combined; in bombers alone it set a production quota of 500 to 600 planes annually.

Of all aircraft, the fighter plane particularly taxed design and technology. As Polikarpov pointed out at a meeting of Soviet designers and Air

Designer Andrei N. Tupolev demonstrates the strength of his latest creation, the all-metal ANT-4 twin-engined bomber of 1925, by standing on its corrugated aluminum wing. The innovative Tupolev later mated the ANT-4's wings and tail to a new fuselage to create the ANT-9 airliner, the first Soviet craft capable of carrying more than 30 passengers.

At a factory where his aircraft were built, Nikolai Polikarpov (left) belatedly learns to fly a trainer in 1934. As chief of Soviet fighter design in the 1930s, Polikarpov concentrated on highly maneuverable but relatively slow biplanes—no match for the swift Luftwaffe monoplanes that were pitted against them at the start of World War II.

Force commanders, a fighter had to be maneuverable and therefore required great power, but extra power would make it heavy and thus difficult to maneuver. Polikarpov had produced a couple of models that were too sluggish, and Grigorovich had created some that were too heavy to fly at all; several prototypes were no sooner airborne than they crashed. Both men were arrested and charged with "conspiring to sabotage the aircraft industry."

By the time of their arraignment, about 600,000 Russians were interned in at least six prison camps. Among them were perhaps 400 designers, engineers and technicians, enough to staff a special "internee design bureau" that had been set up at a former hotel annexed to NKVD headquarters. Polikarpov and Grigorovich were given a team of draftsmen and ordered to get to work. Bizarre as it was, the tactic succeeded. Within eight months, Grigorovich, Polikarpov and their 40 teammates had produced the VT, the fighter Stalin so badly wanted.

The VT was no beauty; it was a little biplane with a stubby fuselage and wings no longer than 20 feet. Neither was it notable for speed; it achieved only 178 miles an hour, about 10 miles an hour short of the speed at which American Curtiss Hawks and British Bulldogs could fly. But the plane had other qualities that more than made up for those defects. It climbed at a rate of 1,600 feet per minute, reached an altitude of 26,500 feet and responded obediently to a flick of the controls. No less an officer than Yakov Alksnis, then deputy chief of the Air Force, took a turn in the cockpit to test the craft himself and pronounced it first-rate. As word of its virtues spread, other high-ranking officials came to the airfield adjoining the factory to see the plane put through its paces. Stalin was among them. He changed the designation from VT to I-5 (the I signifying Istrebitel, "fighter"), ordered the plane put into production and rewarded Polikarpov and Grigorovich with their freedom.

While the need for fighters was causing the Kremlin such concern, bomber design was moving forward apace—thanks partly to the fact that bombers did not present quite such confounding problems as fighters. Bombers were of necessity big, and the bigger the plane the more power it needed. But bombers required neither the speed nor the maneuverability of fighters. Instead, the designer's problems were ones of size and range: how to build planes to take useful payloads, and how to send them over increasingly longer distances. Russian designers had no trouble meeting those demands, and while the decade was still young they had built the world's most gargantuan aircraft—planes that set records for wingspan, power, tonnage and carrying capacity, and for hurdling such obstacles to human and mechanical endurance as the Arctic.

The inventive mind that made the record-breaking aircraft possible was that of Andrei N. Tupolev, a former student of the great scholar Nikolai Zhukovsky. In the course of a distinguished career that spanned nearly half a century, Tupolev was to design more than 100 different aircraft—a feat that itself would be a record. He began modestly in

1921 with the ANT-1. The letters signified his own initials; the plane was a single-seater sports plane with a top speed of 62 miles per hour. Three designs and four years later, working at TsAGI—the Central Institute of Aerodynamics—he completed the ANT-4, a twin-engined heavy bomber that was almost as large as the celebrated *Ilya Muromets* and twice as powerful. With its 97-foot wingspan and 60-foot fuselage, the ANT-4 was so big that to get it out to the airfield for testing, the workmen had to knock down the walls of TsAGI's assembly area. In flight tests, it flew at an undistinguished 103 miles an hour, but it could carry 2,000 pounds of bombs and enough fuel to give it a range of more than 600 miles. It was ordered into mass production and became a mainstay of the Red Air Force; in the next seven years, 216 ANT-4s would be built.

Serviceable though it was in its own right, the ANT-4 was almost more important for the generation of giant bombers it sired. Five years after the ANT-4, Tupolev produced the ANT-6, with four engines instead of two and a bombload of 10,000 pounds. The ANT-6 went into production in 1932, and by the time it was phased out in 1937, more than 800 had been delivered to the Air Force. The ANT series was to go all the way up to No. 42 by 1938, when the last of the line could fly 186 miles an hour with a bombload of more than 8,000 pounds.

Meanwhile, annual production figures for all types of planes were increasing dramatically. In 1930, the Soviet Union produced about 860 aircraft; only two years later production was sufficient to bring the Air Force strength to 2,500 frontline combat planes.

By now Soviet air power had surpassed that of any Western nation. The United States armed forces came closest; in June 1932 the U.S. counted 1,709 aircraft. But in Great Britain in 1933, the Royal Air Force had scarcely 850 aircraft; of those only 488 were available for defense, and all were biplanes that represented hardly any improvement in performance over the types built during World War I.

Germany reported no planes at all that year but two years later made a sudden leap into the public's consciousness when in March 1935 Chancellor Adolf Hitler summarily proclaimed the existence of the Luftwaffe and gave it an instant strength of 1,888 aircraft. Production had taken place secretly in defiance of the strictures of the Versailles Treaty, and much of the newborn Luftwaffe's strength came from craft that had masqueraded as the property of flying clubs and police units.

The Soviet Union, far from concealing its advances, was eager to advertise them to all the world. Massed formations of its burgeoning Air Force regularly appeared in the annual holiday flypasts; on May Day 1932 nine brand-new ANT-6s flew over Moscow, together with 70 ANT-4s, 59 reconnaissance bombers and 27 I-5 fighters. To press the point abroad, Stalin sent the big bombers on exhibition tours to Berlin, Paris, Rome, even to distant Tokyo. Stalin held up the fliers as ideals of the "new Soviet man." He showered them with medals and made a great show of admitting them to the sanctum of his office to plan flights. "So,"

Displaying both Soviet and American flags, the Land of the Soviets is surrounded by newsmen and sightseers during a stopover in Detroit on its celebrated journey from Moscow to New York City in October 1929. The massive heavy bomber first flew to Siberia, then lumbered nonstop across 5,000 miles of the Pacific Ocean to the American West Coast.

he said with heavy humor to one trio of veteran fliers about to set off on a transpolar flight, "the earth is not good enough for you? You want to fly again?" Stalin often saw his heroes off at the airport and was usually on hand to greet them when they returned from successful missions.

During the mid-1930s, Soviet exploits were the sensation of the aviation world. But in May 1935, a calamity occurred that was as embarrassing as it was needless. The greatest plane in the skies was Andrei Tupolev's *Maxim Gorky (pages 50-51)*—the colossal eight-engined transport built in 1934 and used expressly for the purpose of carrying Communist propaganda throughout the Soviet Union. After 11 months of flying displays over scores of Russian cities, the *Maxim Gorky* embarked on a special performance at Tushino Airfield outside Moscow. The purpose of this flight was to make a documentary film about the *Gorky* for showing in schools, aero clubs and factories throughout the U.S.S.R. and abroad. To demonstrate how many passengers the great plane could carry, 44 people were on board; quite a few were TsAGI engineers and technicians being rewarded with a sightseeing ride, and with them were their families.

Flying behind the *Maxim Gorky* was an R-5 observation plane with the documentary cameraman aboard, and alongside—for the purpose of emphasizing the giant's size—was a diminutive I-5 fighter. The fighter's pilot, one Nikolai Blagin, was known as something of a show-off.

The planes had not been long aloft when the pilot of the *Gorky* noticed that Blagin was maneuvering too close to the port wing and radioed a request that the fighter "please veer off to a safer distance."

Blagin's retort came crackling through the earphones: "I'll show you how good a flier I am." With that, he began a loop around the wing of the giant *Gorky*. Up and over he went. And then, to the horror of thousands of spectators below, Blagin's engine stalled. For one breathless moment, the fighter hung suspended upside down—before hurtling into the *Gorky's* wing. The impact tore loose one of the *Gorky's* engines. The fighter remained jammed in position for a few seconds, and then broke loose—to smash against the *Maxim Gorky's* rudder. With a shudder the giant aircraft rolled over and began to disintegrate in midair. The *Gorky's* passengers and crew were flung out into the hazy spring sky at an altitude of 2,300 feet. There were no survivors.

But that debacle was quickly forgotten in a spate of new Soviet records—accompanied by the kettledrums of Soviet propaganda. Throughout 1935 and 1936 Stalin's "Falcons," as he called them, broke more than half a dozen records for altitude previously held by France and Italy; and in May 1937 they achieved a spectacular world first, landing a plane at the North Pole. For that particular achievement the government regaled the public with daily broadcasts detailing the expedition. Said one message from the fliers: "We gathered under an open sky but we didn't feel the cold, wrapped as we were in the glowing words pulsating with the concern of the great Stalin."

The supreme triumph came in August 1937, when three of Stalin's celebrated Falcons—Valery Chkalov, Georgi Baidukov and Alexander Beliakov—made aeronautical history by pioneering a transpolar air route between Europe and North America. Their craft was a Tupolev, of course, the ANT-25, a huge, mothlike monoplane with a single engine and enormous wings filled with fuel. Taking off from Moscow, the fliers remained aloft for an incredible 62½ hours, and when they touched down it was in Vancouver, Washington, after a nonstop flight of 5,507 miles. Their feat captivated Americans no less than Russians; when the fliers reached the East Coast on their way home, they were treated to a presidential reception at the White House and paeans of praise that rivaled those showered on Charles Lindbergh after his conquest of the Atlantic 10 years before.

For Chkalov, alas, celebrity was short-lived. Within the year, he fell victim to the terrible odds of his occupation; testing a new Polikarpov fighter, he experienced an engine failure at low altitude and brushed a telegraph pole while attempting an emergency landing. The plane cartwheeled and Chkalov was hurled from the cockpit, striking his head on a cable drum. He died en route to a hospital; his body lay in state and was then entombed in the Kremlin wall, an honor reserved for state dignitaries and national heroes of the highest order.

The transpolar mission of Chkalov and his comrades was double-edged, as were most Soviet aeronautical endeavors. While waging peace, the Soviets were ever mindful of war: The nation that spanned the Pole might as easily send bombers to any city in Europe. Indeed,

even then the Red Air Force was exercising its ranks and testing its technology on the battlefields of the Spanish Civil War.

The War had erupted in July 1936 as a struggle between a leftist, antimonarchial government and a coalition of rightist groups seeking to restore King Alfonso XIII to the throne and secure power for themselves. The political issues had quickly polarized much of Europe. As the first serious conflict of arms in the West since World War I, the events in Spain had compelling interest for military men in general and airmen in particular. Luftwaffe commander Hermann Göring put it baldly when he called the War an opportunity "to test my young Luftwaffe in this or that technical respect." And so, when the rightist, or Nationalist, leader Generalissimo Francisco Franco appealed for aid to Germany's Adolf Hitler and Italy's Benito Mussolini, both dictators readily obliged.

Franco had marshaled 20,000 troops for a drive on Madrid, but they were stranded in Spanish Morocco, across the Strait of Gibraltar from the southern coast of Spain. Hitler came to the rescue by providing 30 Junkers 52 transports and Luftwaffe crews to fly them; delivering Franco's troops from Morocco to Seville and Cádiz, they carried out the first great strategic airlift in history. The Germans stayed on to grow into the famed Condor Legion, 16,000 men who at their peak would have a frontline strength of 285 aircraft flying in the cause of Franco. For his part, Mussolini sent 12 Savoia 81 transports; they were the first of a total of 763 planes and 50,000 men that Italy was to supply during the War.

For Stalin the conflict in Spain posed a dilemma. Though Communist sympathies were ardently Republican, as the leftist regime was known, Stalin dared not risk any immediate overt action. At the time, he was courting the good will of Britain and France, and both those nations were espousing a policy of nonintervention. Neither was Stalin anxious to provoke Hitler, his likeliest enemy in the event of a European war. Yet if he ignored the cry for help from fellow leftists, he would lose credibility with friend and foe alike. Stalin therefore dissembled. On August 29 he prohibited the export of Soviet military equipment to Spain—and a few days later he secretly authorized the dispatch of aircraft, munitions and men to Spain to support the Republican government.

The aviation contingent numbered 141 pilots and included many of the Red Air Force's highest-ranking and most skilled airmen. In charge was Yakov Smushkevich, a Lithuanian who had entered the Air Force as a political commissar. The pilots selected to gain experience in Spain were the cream of the crop and were rotated in and out on six-month tours of duty. But those facts were not known until much later. The Russians went to Spain on tourists' passports and there adopted *noms de guerre* to conceal their identities. Smushkevich took advantage of a rumor that Americans were on hand and dubbed himself "General Douglas." Others took more Spanish-sounding names such as "Comrade Pablo"—in reality a 25-year-old Ukranian named Pavel Rychagov, who was to distinguish himself as an ace with 15 kills to his credit.

Despite all the camouflage, Russia's military involvement did not

Decked out in full flying regalia, Soviet pilot T. P. Stefanovski looks across an airfield crammed with UT-1 trainers during a public aviation day in 1938. Stefanovski was famous as the test pilot who flew the big TB-3 bombers that carried parasite fighters on their backs.

long remain secret. Newspaper correspondents noted on October 13, 1936, that the Soviet freighter *Bolshevik* put into Cartagena harbor in southern Spain and unloaded 18 I-15 fighters—maneuverable and speedy (225 miles an hour) craft designed by Polikarpov. By the end of the month the reporters had counted the arrival of a dozen vessels and the delivery of about 50 planes. Before long, Soviet fighters and bombers were flying from bases near Madrid, Barcelona, Murcia, Cartagena, Valencia, Albacete, Baeza and Estremadura—locations that formed a network over the entire country.

The first aerial action took place in the skies above Madrid, where German and Italian reconnaissance planes were boldly engaged in scouting missions for Franco. When an Italian Ro-37 reconnaissance plane escorted by two Fiat C.R.32 fighters appeared over Madrid's Manzanares River on November 4, a formation of 10 I-15 biplanes, led by "Comrade Pablo," scrambled to intercept. The Russians sent both Italian fighters down in flames. However, the Ro-37 escaped and reported that the attackers were American Curtiss biplanes. But that error in identification was soon rectified as more and more Soviet aircraft arrived to battle the Germans and Italians for control of Spanish airspace. By midwinter 1937, Soviet air strength in Spain totaled 433 aircraft, mainly I-15s, but with increasing numbers of I-16s, swift little monoplanes that were the first fighters to have retractable landing gear *(page 134)*. So great was the Soviet build-up that it accounted for more

Soviet mechanics assemble I-15 fighters in a secret factory in Alicante during the Spanish Civil War. All told, 1,409 warplanes were shipped to Spain aboard Soviet freighters; many were flown in combat by Red Air Force pilots serving under pseudonyms with the Spanish Republican Army.

*Squadron Commander Yakov Smushkevich
—the "General Douglas" who headed
the Soviet air group in Spain—meets with
some of his pilots at the airfield of Alcañiz
in 1937. The Soviets not only sent pilots and
planes to aid the Spanish Republicans
but also trained Spanish pilots in Russia.*

than 90 per cent of the Republicans' air strength and enabled the Republicans to outnumber the rebel Nationalists by 2 to 1.

For a time, the Soviets also outperformed their German and Italian opponents. "The Heinkel 51 fighter was definitely inferior in speed and firepower to the Red I-15s and I-16s," wrote the Duke of Lerma, who as a 26-year-old Spanish pilot flew 68 bombing missions in German Junkers for Franco's forces. As for the Italian Fiat, the Duke rated the I-15 again superior in firepower, though perhaps with less ceiling.

All through the winter of 1937, the Republicans and Nationalists and their allies fought an aerial war of growing intensity. German and Italian bombing of Republican supply depots—and civilian population centers—reached a level unimagined in World War I. Against such tactics, the Republicans sent up swarms of Soviet fighters. At one point in February, the Duke of Lerma was part of a formation of Junkers on a mission against Republican supply lines east of Madrid. "The closer we got to enemy lines, the grimmer the scene looked," wrote the Duke. "Red fighters seemed to fill the sky, waiting to pounce on us as we approached in our slow, dignified Junkers." He made two runs at his target, plowing through the fighters only to be "met each time by a concentrated barrage of flak. It was a most impressive and hair-raising experience; we had seen nothing like it before." He finally succeeded in reaching his target on the third run—but emerged with a severely damaged plane. "My machine was vibrating from nose to tail, shaking herself to pieces," he wrote. "It had been very difficult to concentrate on my bombing, for I instinctively wanted to grab my machine gun and rake the I-16s weaving in and out of our bombers."

By midsummer it was not unusual for 90 aircraft to be swirling and screaming through the sky in a single battle. And on one day in October the Republican/Soviet Air Force mounted no fewer than 400 sorties against the enemy. Meanwhile, in Moscow, Stalin, though still maintaining a façade of neutrality, was publicly decorating Soviet fliers for valor in Spain. Into the pantheon of Heroes of the Soviet Union went 17 veterans of the Civil War combat. Among them were "Comrade Pablo" Rychagov and two other triple aces.

Yet for all the Soviet numbers and heroics, the balance of strength was slowly shifting, and the Red Air Force would soon find itself at an unnerving disadvantage in the air. Göring had meant what he said when he spoke of Spain as a test for the Luftwaffe. German officers, reviewing every move of every engagement, had been pondering principles of combat. German engineers had been feverishly improving the design of German aircraft. By July 1937 German factories were ready with a new model, the Messerschmitt 109, a deadly little machine that represented a quantum leap in aerial technology: It could fly almost 100 miles an hour faster than the Soviet I-15s and I-16s.

The entry of the Messerschmitts into the air war in Spain was a debacle for the Red Air Force. In August, the Me 109s shot down 60 Red aircraft west of Madrid. In the first few days of September they shot down another 30 over Saragossa. And the Me 109s were only the most conspicuous of a whole new fleet the Germans were committing to combat. During the summer the Germans also introduced the Heinkel 111 and Dornier 17 bombers, which carried 3,330-pound and 1,650-pound bombloads respectively—vast improvements over the 660 pounds the earlier Heinkel 70s had carried. In December the Germans brought on the Junkers 87A, the first of the screaming dive bombers.

In addition to improving design, the Germans were also applying the tactical lessons of combat. They discovered that to go into battle three by three, as airmen had done since World War I, was self-defeating; pilots concentrated more on keeping formation than on anticipating the enemy's moves. The Luftwaffe shifted to the *Rotte* and the *Schwarm*—groups of two and four respectively. That way they could fly in teams that were equally capable of offensive and defensive fighting, with one plane always providing cover for another. In threesomes, if one plane maneuvered to defend a second, the third was left on its own.

As air operations continued into 1938, Soviet losses mounted into the hundreds and air superiority slipped from the Red Air Force's grasp. By summer, it was no longer an effective instrument, and the Kremlin ordered a withdrawal. By the end of the year all Soviet personnel had returned home. When they departed, they left to the Spanish Republicans what remained of their aircraft. But that was precious little. Of the 1,409 planes supplied to Spain between October 1936 and the end of 1938, a dismaying 1,176—or 83 per cent—had been destroyed.

Throughout 1938, pilots, commanders and other personnel returning from Spain were welcomed as heroes and decorated at holiday parades. But behind the scenes, Soviet authorities were agonizing over the Spanish misadventure. For one thing, air commanders had found no use for the huge, long-range ANT bombers so zealously built during the decade. It was true, of course, that Spain was a battlefield of restricted distances. Nevertheless the developing pattern of air combat

Soviet mechanics prepare an I-16 fighter for takeoff at a Spanish air base in June 1938. The contraption mounted atop the truck was an ingenious homemade starting device; the rod was connected to the vehicle's drive shaft, which supplied enough power to turn over the plane's engine.

A formation of Soviet I-16 fighters flies low over a grassy field in Spain in June of 1937. The nimble little craft was called Mosca, or housefly, by the Spanish Republicans, and called Rata—rat—by the Nationalists and their German allies.

seemed—for the moment at least—to be running against high-altitude area bombing in favor of more or less low-level, pinpoint support of ground forces. The planes required fell somewhere between the giant, long-range ANTs and the diminutive I-15 and I-16 fighters—that is to say, aircraft on the order of the Luftwaffe's He 111, Do 17 and Ju 87. "What happened came as an unpleasant, one might even say an inexplicable, surprise," aircraft designer Alexander Yakovlev later reflected. "Yet there it was: We were definitely lagging behind Hitler's Germany, our potential adversary. Those celebrated record-breaking planes and giants of the air were nowhere near what we needed."

One way or another, everyone sought a scapegoat. The men blamed the planes. Commanding officers blamed the men, charging them with lack of initiative in combat and poor standards of flying and marksmanship. Stalin blamed everybody—men, officers and designers—and used the defeat in Spain as an excuse to intensify the police control that had put Polikarpov and Grigorovich in prison at the start of the decade.

Since 1930, the secret police had extended its grasp over every aspect of Soviet society. By the mid-1930s the number of prisoners had multiplied tenfold to an estimated six million—and for many of those, prison was merely a way station. In 1937 Stalin unleashed what one Soviet diplomat later termed "a mad bacchanalia of executions." Uncounted thousands were slaughtered; at one prison alone executions took place twice a week, in groups of 40 or more victims at a time.

No quarter of Soviet life was harder hit by the purges than the Air Force. The purge struck with full force on the evening of November 23, 1937, when Yakov Alksnis, the commanding general, was arrested while on his way to a diplomatic reception in Moscow. He was accused of treason and sent to Lubyanka prison in Moscow. His arrest was utterly inexplicable to the airmen under his command; he had received the Order of the Red Star only the year before, when he had had the distinction of leading the May Day flypast over Red Square. Once he was arrested, he vanished from sight. It was rumored that he was brutally tortured; the *Great Soviet Encyclopedia* records that he was shot on July 29, 1938. Joining him in oblivion were his deputy, Vasili Khripin; A. I. Todorsky, head of the Zhukovsky Air Force Academy; seven of the senior Air Force commanders; and five military-district air commanders. The purges continued throughout that year and the next, until, by the end of 1939, 75 per cent of the senior officers had been removed from command and most of them had been executed.

The extent and severity of the purges was stunning. The shadow of the NKVD had always loomed over the Air Force, and every officer knew that even the most casual remark could blight a career. A pilot named Vladimir Unishevsky later recalled how he came to grief one evening among two close friends. He was enrolled in a commanders' course at an air base near Sevastopol in 1934 when Sergei Kirov, one of Stalin's closest associates, was assassinated. One evening not long afterward Unishevsky was in a recreation hall with his friends, "talking about the murder as usual," when he remarked in jest that some people would have been pleased had it been Stalin who was murdered instead of Kirov. Everyone laughed and the subject was dropped.

Later that evening Unishevsky was summoned before the secret police and bluntly asked if he had ever indulged in anti-Soviet propaganda. The question came as such a surprise that he laughed. But it was no joke. Unishevsky was dismissed from the Air Force on the ground of "political unsuitability" and consigned to flying for the mail service. He concluded that one of his two friends must have been an informer.

"The worst thing that can happen to an officer is to be dismissed on the grounds of political and moral unsuitability," Unishevsky later explained. "Every official is prejudiced against him from the start; if he puts in for certain posts and occupations, he is automatically turned down." Four years later, facing a life of unremitting harassment, Unishevsky stole a plane from a local flying club and fled to the West.

He was one of the fortunate few. For those in critical positions, escape was next to impossible. In the aircraft industry an estimated 450 designers and engineers were arrested between 1934 and 1941. Of those, about 100 died in labor camps and 50 were executed.

Even the great Tupolev, who had become the head of all aviation

In this dramatic sequence of photographs recording the clash of major powers in Spain, a German Messerschmitt 109 fighter (top right) prepares to swoop down on a pair of Soviet SB-2 bombers. One of the bombers is hit, bursts into flames and plummets to earth, where it explodes upon impact (bottom), leaving a trail of dark smoke to mark its descent.

design, fell under Stalin's wrath and was sentenced to life imprisonment, beginning in 1937. In his case, the mind-boggling charge was that he had sold Germany the original plans from which the Messerschmitt 109 had been developed. The accusation would have been laughable had it not been so diabolical. Prodigious worker that he was, Tupolev went right on designing; and one of his craft, a high-speed bomber designated the Tu-2, won him a prize and the unexpected mercy of Stalin. In December 1943 the dictator summoned Tupolev before him for the extraordinary experience of being given a handshake by way of apology—a concession no other person is known to have been accorded by the stubborn Stalin. But by that time Russia was in combat with the Germans, and presumably not even Stalin's distrust blinded him to Tupolev's peerless value to the aviation industry.

It is astonishing, given this atmosphere of madness and murder, that the Air Force could respond at all to the critical demands placed upon it in the late 1930s and early 1940s. One such crisis occurred in 1939 on the eastern fringes of the U.S.S.R. when a band of Mongolian nomads inadvertently provoked a brief but bloody border war with the Japanese occupiers of Manchuria. In May of that year, when the Mongolian nomads migrated east across the Khalkhin-Gol River, they were driven back by border guards from the Japanese Kwantung Army. A number of skirmishes followed, and soon the Soviets and the Japanese were engaged in a summer-long fight for a strip of arid pastureland between the Khalkhin-Gol River and the village of Nomonhan, 10 miles to the east.

From a few shots fired by a handful of troops using light weapons, the conflict escalated into a massive confrontation involving 270,000 men equipped with tanks and heavy artillery, and supported by squadrons of aircraft. In sheer numbers, the armies and air forces engaged were greater even than those in the Spanish Civil War. To command Soviet air operations, the High Command dispatched Yakov Smushkevich, the "General Douglas" of Civil War fame and one of the few veteran officers to survive the purges. He was now—presumably for his political reliability—deputy commander of the Red Air Force. At the front, he was nominally in charge of 515 fighters and twin-engined SB-2 medium bombers—the Soviets having commenced to build ground-attack craft on the German model. He deployed them in massive formations of 60 or more planes against Japanese ground forces on the Nomonhan plateau and sent I-15 and I-16 fighters aloft as escorts. The Japanese responded in kind until at times more than 200 planes were in combat over the wasteland.

The Japanese had nothing to compare with the German Me 109 that had so devastated the Red Air Force during the Spanish Civil War. The Kwantung Army's air force consisted of about 500 aircraft all told, mixed fighters and light bombers, some of Japanese manufacture and others imported from Italy. Among the Japanese fighters were Nakajima 97s, frail craft that were highly maneuverable but undergunned

Soviet fliers in an SB-2 bomber squadron are briefed for a mission by their commander (right) during the Winter War against Finland in 1939-1940.

and perilously vulnerable; their slender frames had no armor and their fuel tanks were carried externally on the wings. The Japanese pilots, however, were highly skilled and well disciplined; they made the most of the Nakajima's maneuverability and often got the better of the Reds.

But soon the Red Air Force was receiving its first I-153 fighters, much-improved versions of the workhorse I-15s. The new craft had two formidable 7.62-millimeter machine guns, 850-horsepower engines that gave them a high rate of climb and, most important, retractable landing gear that enabled them to fly 280 miles an hour—55 miles an hour faster than the I-15s. The retractable landing gear was a novelty in fighter planes, and—so the story goes—the Soviets duped the Japanese by flying into battle with their wheels down, resembling the old I-15s. Then, having lured the enemy into combat, the Soviets retracted their landing gear, increased speed and turned on the Japanese.

More important than gaining the edge in a dogfight, the Red Air Force for the first time showed real skill in coordinating air operations with ground troops. The moving spirit behind what was to become ironclad Soviet doctrine was General Georgi Zhukov, who had served in the Czar's cavalry in 1917 and since then had displayed a talent for whipping troops into shape in short order. Not only a practical man but one with a certain vision as well, he saw more clearly than anyone else the virtue of an air force in close, constant support of infantry, artillery and armor. He arrived in July to take charge of the War and planned a massive strike against the Japanese for August 20. To ensure that everyone knew what to expect and where to expect it, he required all pilots to study the proposed operation jointly with infantry and tank commanders, and to learn the minutest details of terrain, such as hills that could be expected to slow the movement of tanks and defiles that might conceal artillery or masses of troops. Previously, officers had sent their airmen aloft with vague instructions and hopes for the best.

The battle opened at 6 a.m. on August 20, when a Russian force of 100,000 men backed by 1,000 large-caliber artillery pieces launched a furious attack along a 48-mile front. Simultaneously, an enormous formation of aircraft—150 SB-2 bombers escorted by 144 fighters—sallied forth to strafe and bomb enemy positions and prepare the way for 800 Soviet tanks already on the roll. The airmen met little opposition from the Japanese pilots, who were apparently taken completely by surprise. The aerial assault lasted 15 minutes—and no sooner had it ceased than another huge wave of aircraft appeared, this time 52 bombers and 167 escorting fighters. The second group did not stop at the frontline positions but flew on to attack Japanese airfields and troop concentrations in the rear. By the end of the day, the Red Air Force had achieved air superiority over the battlefield, and with its massive aid, Soviet ground forces had overrun the Japanese forward positions.

The battle continued until the end of August, with the Soviets putting unrelenting pressure on the Japanese. In a departure from their favored tactics, the Soviets waged a psychological campaign against the Japanese by sending small groups of bombers over at 20,000 feet to drop their bombs and race for home before Japanese fighters could rise to intercept. The Japanese attempted to counter by mounting fighter patrols at high altitudes, but that tactic had a fatal flaw; the pilots carried insufficient oxygen in their craft and fell prey to hypoxia.

At the other end of the tactical scale, Soviet I-16 fighters tried their wings as low-level ground attackers, flying at treetop height to strafe Japanese positions. In one raid, 50 I-16s swept in on a Japanese air base, shot down the commanding officer as he was taking off on a reconnaissance mission and burned five other aircraft on the ground. Such raids sometimes came in quick succession, five or six within as many hours. The endless alerts soon exhausted the Japanese pilots, whose commanders could not afford the luxury of rotation because too many fliers were engaged elsewhere in Manchuria against the Chinese. By the end of August the Kwantung Army was ready to give up the fight, and on September 16 the two nations signed an armistice.

The claims conflict, but the best estimate is that in three short months of border warfare the Red Air Force destroyed more than 160 Japanese

aircraft while losing about 200 of its own; considering the fact that the Soviets were generally on the offensive, the attrition rate was acceptable. Of even greater significance than the figures was the fact that Soviet airmen had played a significant role in enabling their companion ground forces to frustrate Japanese ambitions in Mongolia. Stalin rewarded 60 of his returning Falcons as Heroes of the Soviet Union.

The cessation of hostilities with Japan came none too soon for the Soviet Union. A far greater menace loomed on September 1, when German tanks smashed into Poland, provoking Great Britain and France to declare war and thus opening World War II. For the Soviet Union, it was a period of accommodation and maneuver. Nine days before the Nazi blitzkrieg Stalin had signed a pact with Hitler dividing Poland into Russian and German "spheres of influence." Its most practical effect was to put a buffer between the two potential enemies. Stalin was thus able to turn his attention to another area where Russia ardently desired "influence," namely Finland.

For many months Soviet Foreign Minister Vyacheslav Molotov had been pressing the Finns to cede to Russia a strip of southern Finland, the better to protect the approaches to Leningrad. The Finns adamantly refused. Negotiations reached an impasse, and on November 30, 1939, Russia invaded Finland.

At first the Soviets seemed to have everything in their favor—not least in the matter of air power. To support ground operations alone they mustered 900 planes. Unfortunately the force was more impressive in size than in quality; the Soviets were so cocky after their eventual success in the Far East that they employed mainly vintage I-15s and I-16s, plus some antiquated bombers. General Smushkevich, the hero of Khalkhin-Gol, was once again in charge of the operation. But not only was he saddled with second-rank aircraft, most of his officers were untested novices. Presumably the Russians did not consider Finland enough of a challenge to engage the Manchuria veterans.

To all appearances, the Finnish Air Force scarcely qualified for the name, mustering only 145 aircraft—a variety of British, German and Italian fighters, and some French Moranes for scouting. With such overwhelming numbers on the Russian side, no one imagined for a moment that the Red Air Force would fail to demolish the Finns at a blow. But neither did anyone imagine how tenaciously and resourcefully the Finns would fight to protect their homeland. The Winter War, as the conflict came to be known, was to be a painful and humiliating experience for the Russians in general and for the Red Air Force in particular. It would take 105 days, until March 13, to snuff out Finnish resistance. And the cost to Russia in men and planes was to be appalling.

The hostilities opened when Soviet bombers roared over the cities of Helsinki, Viipuri and Petsamo in a series of noonday raids. But instead of the abject surrender they had expected, the Russians found the Finns defiantly reporting the raids to the world press. Moscow Radio claimed

A squad of grinning Red Army soldiers, taking part in an imaginative airlift experiment during the Finnish War, peeks out from pods slung under the wings of a ski-equipped R-5 reconnaissance plane. The ribbed fairings hanging beneath the men were swung up and latched to streamline the pods before takeoff.

that the Russian pilots had merely dropped bread to the starving masses in Finland. The Finns had photographs to prove otherwise—the Soviets had bombed the university district and had managed by accident to bomb their own embassy as well. With a humor born of desperation and a stubborn will to survive, the Finns coined a term that would endure throughout the War. Thereafter they contemptuously referred to Russian bombs as "Molotov's breadbaskets."

For the next two weeks, heavy snowstorms obliterated many of the ground targets and brought air operations to a halt. But in the middle of December the weather cleared and the Red Air Force began mounting raids in strength, only to find the Finns undaunted by the numbers and inventive in their opposition. In a terrifying variation on the technique of strafing ground forces, Finnish pilots took to climbing above the Soviet bombers and then diving straight into the middle of the Soviet formations with all machine guns hammering. A singlehanded battle waged by Captain Jorman Sarvanto of the Finns' 24th Squadron was typical.

On January 6, flying a Fokker D-21, he was patrolling the route the Soviet bombers followed to central Finland when seven planes appeared on the horizon. Sarvanto headed toward them, climbed rapidly above the enemy and then dived. At 30 yards he fired a burst that sent one of the bombers spiraling down in a plume of black smoke. The Soviets broke formation and scattered in confusion—enabling him to pick them off seriatim. Whirling around, he dispatched two more bombers in quick succession, withdrew for a moment, then returned to the attack and knocked down three more. The seventh and last, which had headed back toward Russian lines, escaped only because Sarvanto ran out of ammunition. But one of Sarvanto's squadronmates, who had seen the fight from a distance, flew swiftly over and got the last plane.

As Soviet losses began to mount, General Smushkevich ordered more raids to be directed against Finnish airfields. But the Finns were as crafty on the ground as they were ferocious in the air. They had already vacated their air bases and had scattered their planes about the country in carefully camouflaged emergency airstrips.

Even when targets remained in place and could be reached without interception, the Soviet bombers kept missing. Of 60 raids the Soviets launched against the port of Turku, not one seriously disrupted shipping. Moreover, the hard-won lessons of Manchuria seemed to have been forgotten. Perhaps because of the awful weather, with snow and temperatures as low as 30° below zero, the Red Air Force seemed unable to coordinate its actions with the Red Army ground forces, which advanced only at a snail's pace and with great difficulty.

Yet for all their blunders, the Soviets had the advantage of unlimited resources. In January they added 500 aircraft to the front, and among the reinforcements were the new I-153s and late-model I-16s that had proved their worth in Manchuria, plus some new DB-3 bombers, which were the work of the up-and-coming designer Sergei Ilyushin. In February came another 500 Red Air Force machines. Now sheer weight of numbers began to tell against the Finns. On March 13 the Finns could hold out no longer and ceded the Russians the buffer zone they wanted.

The Moscow propaganda machine moved into gear to extol yet another glorious Soviet victory. Stalin decorated 68 fliers as Heroes of the Soviet Union; and he awarded the prestigious Red Banner to one air brigade, 12 air regiments and two squadrons. But the figures told no tale of glory. The Red Air Force had lost between 700 and 900 aircraft—while the Finns had lost no more than 60 or 70.

None of this, of course, escaped Adolf Hitler and his war planners in Berlin. Toward the end of 1940 German intelligence estimated that—between the purges and the losses suffered in Manchuria and Finland—the Red Army and Air Force would require four years to regain the level of efficiency they had enjoyed in 1937. Hitler was delighted. On December 18, 1940, he issued Directive No. 21, Operation *Barbarossa,* a plan to invade the Soviet Union in six months' time.

The Soviets had abundant warnings of German intentions. Incredibly, Stalin refused to heed them. When border guards reported early in winter that the Luftwaffe was making reconnaissance flights over Soviet territory almost daily, he ordered the Red Air Force to ignore the incursions. The flights continued with impunity; in the six months that passed between December 1940 and June 1941 the Luftwaffe carried out 150 such missions.

In February, a German printer with Communist leanings provided the Soviet consulate in Berlin with a slender German-Russian conversation manual that had been printed in vast numbers. It contained such phrases as "Hands up!" "I'll shoot!" and "Surrender." When the intelligence was sent to Moscow, Stalin ordered that this, too, be ignored.

All through the winter and spring the signs proliferated. Early in June came word from an agent in Switzerland that the Germans were planning to invade on June 22. The agent also supplied details of the Wehrmacht order of battle, the initial objectives and the Germans' estimate of possible Soviet responses. At intelligence headquarters in Moscow, Soviet experts decided that the report was too detailed to be true. Later in the month, on the evening of the 18th, a German deserter crossed the border in the district of Kiev. He confessed that he had struck an officer while drunk; he expected to be shot and so was deserting to the Russians with information he thought would assure his welcome—not only the date of the invasion, June 22, but even the hour, 3:15 a.m. The commanding general, following Stalin's line, snorted: "A German fearing for his skin could babble anything."

By the evening of June 21 Soviet guards could hear the rumble of tanks and trucks in the darkness as German forces took up their positions all along the borders that separated Russia from Poland and Rumania. Messages to that effect poured into the Soviet High Command throughout the evening. But when Stalin was told, he accused the High Command of "creating panic for no reason."

3
The struggle for survival

The German ground and air commanders were at loggerheads. The Wehrmacht's Field Marshal Fedor von Bock, whose Army Group Center would bear the brunt of the fighting, insisted that Operation *Barbarossa*—the Nazi invasion of Russia—must commence with a great artillery barrage during the last lingering hour of darkness.

Ideally, the bombardment would have been accompanied by the Luftwaffe striking forward enemy airfields with all its might. But Field Marshal Albert Kesselring, whose Air Fleet 2 was assigned to support Bock, opposed the timetable. "My groups," said Kesselring, "need daylight to get into formation and attack in force. If the Army persists in marching in darkness, it will be a whole hour before we can be over the enemy's airfields, and by then the birds will have flown."

The two finally compromised: History's most massive assault would be launched by a handful of bombers with elite crews especially trained for night operations. Incongruous in their scanty number, a mere 30 Heinkel 111s, Junkers 88s and Dornier 17Zs would cross the frontier in darkness, flying at high altitude. Then, in groups of three, they would swoop out of what little remained of the year's shortest night, attacking 10 advanced Soviet airfields between Bialystok and Lvov, mostly within the huge salient created by Russia's 1939 seizure of eastern Poland.

The purpose of the pioneer planes, far from attempting to pulverize the Soviet Air Force, was simply to buy time for the main Luftwaffe assault by spreading terror and confusion. In that, they succeeded.

The Russians were taken utterly unawares. Stalin himself had given assurances that war with Nazi Germany was impossible; the belated order for Soviet aircraft to be dispersed had not yet reached the forward bases; many air and ground crews were away on weekend leave, while most of those who remained were slumbering. Their planes were parked wing tip to wing tip in tidy array on the airfields toward which the bombers bearing the black cross of the Luftwaffe now descended.

It was precisely 3:15 a.m. on Sunday, June 22, 1941.

Sweeping low over their targets, the attackers disgorged hundreds of four-pound SD-2 fragmentation bombs whose incandescent shards

Wrecked I-16 fighters litter one of the 66 Soviet airfields devastated by the massive Luftwaffe surprise attack in the opening hours of Operation Barbarossa on the 22nd of June, 1941.

shredded fuselages and tore open fuel tanks, allowing floods of blazing gasoline to escape and spread from plane to plane until entire airfields were engulfed by oceans of flame. After their first run, the bombers turned for another pass, this time strafing by the light of the pyres they had created.

Then the invaders wheeled back toward the west, whence they had come. Not a shot had been fired against them. Near Rovno, south of the Pripet Marshes, a Russian air commander surveyed the wreckage of his planes—and wept.

The entire attack had lasted only a few minutes. During that same teardrop of time, the 2,000-mile-long frontier from the chilly Baltic to the warm Black Sea blazed with the fire of some 6,000 guns; about 1,500 tanks rumbled from their starting points, and more than 3,800,000 German soldiers set forth toward a grim destiny in the east.

Operation *Barbarossa* had begun.

The Luftwaffe's main force would strike at sunrise with 500 high-level bombers, 270 dive bombers and 480 fighters. Yet despite their formidable strength, the German fliers were seriously outnumbered: Official statistics conflict, but it has been knowledgeably estimated that the Red Air Force possessed as many as 7,500 aircraft in the western military districts, with another 4,500 to 5,000 in the interior and in the Far East, where the Japanese presented a continuing threat.

Those numbers were deceptive, however. By almost every other measurement the Luftwaffe held a clear advantage. Most important, *Barbarossa* caught the Soviet air arm in the midst of sweeping changes in organization, equipment, training and airfield facilities.

As early as July 1940, the Soviets had begun—at least on paper—a wholesale restructuring of their air force, with regiments of 60 to 64 aircraft apiece replacing squadrons of 20 to 30 planes as the basic tactical units. From three to five regiments would constitute an air division. Most of the air divisions would, in turn, be attached directly to—and take their orders from—ground armies.

The general aim was to enhance cooperation between the air and ground forces. But the complex reorganization was far from complete. Of 106 new air regiments authorized in February 1941, scarcely 19 had actually been formed. As a result, few ground armies had as yet received their own air divisions. Soviet air operations were a complete muddle, both in command and assignment.

Similarly, a new generation of combat aircraft had just started to reach the border units. The sorry showing of the Soviet Air Force in the later stages of the Spanish Civil War had proved beyond doubt that the old Polikarpov I-15 and I-16 fighters were obsolescent; not even the I-153s, which had performed well enough against Japanese aircraft in Mongolia, could match the German Messerschmitt in speed and in diving and climbing capabilities. Yet the machines remained in frontline squadrons.

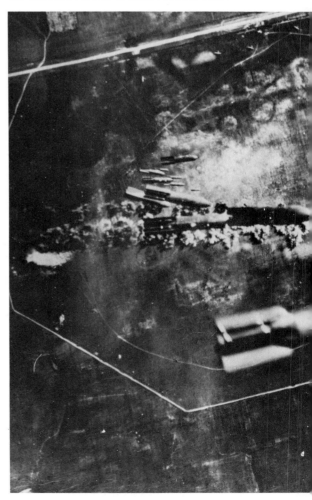

A stick of 500-pound German bombs, their fins fitted with terror-inducing sirens, rains down on a Soviet airfield at Vilna during the Barbarossa attack. Other bombs can be seen blasting a cratered path across the field, where some of the parked aircraft are visible as white specks below the main road at top and near the two hangars at upper right.

Moreover, the Red Air Force's twin-engined SB-2 and DB-3 bombers were not only inferior in almost every aspect of their performance to the Luftwaffe's Ju 88 and He 111, but were deemed outdated in their doctrinal role—as experience in Spain had shown. They were being replaced by lighter, faster machines whose primary purpose was to provide close support for ground forces.

As with fighters, however, the transition was tortuously slow. By June 22, 1941, and the onslaught of *Barbarossa*, only 20 per cent of the Red Air Force had been equipped with new planes—whose air and ground crews were still struggling to learn how to handle them.

Perhaps worst of all, the new as well as the old aircraft had been placed in dire jeopardy by feckless policy decisions. Far from using his recently acquired territories in eastern Poland and the Baltic states as buffer space to be traversed by the invading Germans, Stalin had simply pushed forward his own military frontiers. As one calamitous result, according to the Soviet *History of the Great Patriotic War,* many airfields "had been built much too close to the frontier, which made them specially vulnerable in the event of a surprise attack."

Because airfields in the occupied lands were both few in number and primitive in quality, an enormous construction and expansion program was begun in the spring of 1941—and the NKVD was placed in charge of the work. With an abundance of forced labor at its disposal but with woefully little understanding of military requirements, the Soviet police organization, ignoring the pleas of air commanders, insisted that the entire project be undertaken simultaneously rather than in carefully planned stages.

Thus, instead of being prudently dispersed on June 22, thousands of Russian planes were massed on the relatively few already operational fields. Against those inviting targets the first great wave of German aircraft flew on a mission that, as defined by the order for *Barbarossa,* was brutally simple: Attacking with sledge-hammer strength, the Luftwaffe would "paralyze" the Soviet Air Force and "put it out of commission."

In the event, the measure of the mission's success would dictate the course of the conflict during the first crucial months of the Red Air Force's monumental struggle to survive.

During that frightful phase, which ended only when the antagonists—almost equally exhausted by the battle for Moscow—paused to draw breath for the ordeals yet to come, the Red Air Force clung to existence by the slenderest of threads. Yet virtually unnoticed amid the staggering statistics of Soviet losses was the fact that the Luftwaffe itself was suffering a rate of attrition from which it would never fully recover.

In several striking ways, patterns were set in the first few weeks that would endure throughout the rest of the War. Perhaps most significant, both sides committed themselves to the employment of aviation as a tactical rather than a strategic weapon. Hitler's orders were most explicit. After the destruction of the Soviet Air Force, the Führer decreed, the Luftwaffe's "highest priority must be given to the direct support of the ground forces. Attacks against industrial centers must not be made until the ground troops have achieved their operational goals."

The Soviets were equally dedicated to using their aircraft as a sort of artillery with wings. "In Stalinist military theory," wrote a top Air Force general, "it is considered that victory in contemporary war is attained only by direct assistance to the ground forces in all types of operations." Added another Russian airman: "Air superiority is not an end in itself, but is for the benefit of ground troops."

And so, wherever and whenever men fought and bled on Soviet soil, swarms of planes were sure to be clashing close overhead. Much of the air war was fought below 2,000 feet, and a battle, as witnessed from a distance by a German pilot, appeared as "a black, pulsating mass of insects boiling up over a huge grass fire."

Even as the 30 German pioneers neared their home bases on June 22, the main Luftwaffe armada was airborne and heading implacably for the streaks of dawn now appearing on the eastern horizon. Incredibly, even after the pioneer raids, the Soviet Air Force remained inert. So inhibited were Red air commanders by Stalin's steel grip that, in the absence of orders from Moscow, scarcely a single Russian plane took to the sky.

"We hardly believed our eyes," recalled Captain Hans von Hahn, commander of a Luftwaffe group that attacked in the Lvov area. "Row after row of reconnaissance planes, bombers and fighters stood lined up as if on parade." For 20 leisurely minutes, the attackers passed back and forth over the airfield, smashing nearly 100 planes of all types with cannon and machine-gun fire at a token cost of two Messerschmitts slightly damaged by antiaircraft fire.

The same gladdening sight greeted German fliers at 66 airfields along the entire frontier. And even in the rare instances where the Russians reacted, they did so to no good effect. Near Brest-Litovsk, 30 Soviet fighters tried to take off; German planes swept over them, dropped a lethal cluster of fragmentation bombs in their midst and left them blazing at the end of the runway—still in formation.

By 4:30 a.m., most of the invading aircraft were already back at their bases—refueling and rearming for the next strike. With only two of their number missing, they had left behind a flaming vista of destruction—and hapless turmoil. "We are being fired on," a Soviet border unit had wired to a higher command. "What shall we do?" The reply: "You must be insane. And why is your signal not in code?" At Riga, when the Red Army district headquarters asked for assistance from an air unit at Libau, the response was despairing: "Can give no support. My fighter regiment has been destroyed by bombs."

Moscow was no help whatsoever. While the first bombs were falling, Admiral N. G. Kuznetsov, the People's Commissar of the Navy, was catnapping on a couch in his office. He was abruptly awakened by a telephone call from the commander of the Black Sea Fleet with the electrifying news: "An air raid has been carried out against Sevastopol. Antiaircraft artillery is fighting off the attack. Several bombs have fallen on the city."

Kuznetsov excitedly called Stalin's office, where a duty officer named Loginev somewhat laconically told him: "Comrade Stalin is not here, and I don't know where he is."

Kuznetsov: "I have an exceedingly important message, which I must immediately relay to Comrade Stalin personally."

Loginev: "I can't help you in any way."

And that was that.

Only at 5:30 a.m.—after the German Ambassador to Moscow had delivered a message that was tantamount to a declaration of war—did Stalin at last become convinced that he had been betrayed by Adolf Hitler, his partner in Polish infamy. Even then, it was not until 7:15—four hours after *Barbarossa* had begun—that the Soviet dictator allowed Defense Commissar Semyon Timoshenko to send an order for the Red Air Force to take the offensive and "destroy the enemy aircraft with powerful blows."

By then, for what was left of the world's most numerous air force, the command was tragic in its absurdity.

Throughout that sunny Sunday, the Luftwaffe came in clouds. German fighters and bombers flew repeated sorties. Within the first few hours, columns of oily black smoke towered over airfields in the areas of Kiev, Riga, Kaunas, Vilna, Grodno, Zhitomir and Sevastopol. General I. V. Boldin, first deputy commander of the Western Military District, was witness of the extent to which the Luftwaffe seized command of the Soviet skies.

Attempting to fly from Minsk to Bialystok to regain contact with the Tenth Army, Boldin surveyed a spectacle of ruin. "Trains and warehouses were burning," he wrote later. "Ahead and to the left of us there were big fires on the horizon. Enemy bombers were continuously streaking through the air."

Boldin's plane flew as low as possible, skirting population centers. "The farther we went," he continued, "the worse it became. There were more and more enemy planes in the air. It was impossible to continue the flight. Up ahead there was a small airfield with planes burning beside a metal hangar. I made a decision and signaled the pilot to land." Running for his life, Boldin "heard the roar of motors overhead. Nine Junkers appeared. They came down over the airfield and began bombing. The explosions shook the earth" and destroyed the plane in which Boldin had just landed.

By now, Soviet fliers were fighting back along the entire front, but both airmen and aircraft were hopelessly outclassed. To one German air officer it seemed that the Red Air Force was "nothing but a large and cumbersome instrument of small combat value." On some Soviet aircraft, for example, the gun sight consisted of nothing more than a hand-painted circle on the windscreen. Even a Soviet analyst later admitted that the Russian air response was "uncoordinated and purposeless."

At about 11 a.m. on that first morning of the invasion, a wing of Ju 87 Stuka dive bombers returned to its base north of Warsaw after plastering enemy lines along the Bug River. No sooner had the planes landed than six Soviet SB-2s appeared overhead, lumbering along in close, highly vulnerable formation. Into their midst raced two or three Messerschmitt 109Fs, throttles open and guns blazing.

"As the first fighter fired, thin threads of smoke seemed to join it to the bomber," said Captain Herbert Pabst, a Stuka squadron commander who witnessed the engagement from the ground. He watched enthralled as the bomber rolled to one side and arrowed, engines shrieking, into the ground. A second bomber turned red, then exploded and sent its shards wafting earthward "like great autumnal leaves." Within moments, six separate plumes of smoke reached lazily into the sky. But the bombing attacks were far from over. They continued throughout the afternoon—and out of 21 arrivals, Pabst counted 21 casualties.

Of such doomed bombing efforts, the Luftwaffe's Field Marshal Kesselring would soon say, almost pityingly: "It was infanticide." Yet even during that first day, now and again there was something about the way the Russian bomber and fighter pilots fought that brought faint stirrings of unease to their antagonists. One Luftwaffe colonel had a feeling that the "Soviet pilots were fatalists, fighting without any hope of success or confidence in their own abilities and driven only by their own fanaticism or by fear of their commissars."

An early evidence of that spirit came in a wild dogfight between a flight of Messerschmitts and a group of I-16s over Kobrin. Three Soviet and two German fighters were quickly shot down. Then, as the melee neared its end, Lieutenant Dmitri Kokorev of the 124th Fighter Air Regiment, finding that he had used all his ammunition, hurled his I-16 into a vertical bank—and deliberately rammed a Messerschmitt. The German crashed in flames, but Kokorev somehow got his crippled plane safely back to earth.

Meanwhile, in the vicinity of Zholkva, Lieutenant I. I. Ivanov intentionally drove the propeller of his I-16 into the tail of a Heinkel 111 bomber. For his deed, Ivanov was made a Hero of the Soviet Union—posthumously.

In all, at least nine Soviet pilots resorted to the desperate tactic of ramming during the War's first day. They contributed virtually nothing toward stemming the German avalanche, and by the time the sun vanished behind a smoldering horizon, 1,811 Russian planes had been

The immensity of the battleground stretching 1,750 miles across western Russia from the Arctic to the Black Sea made it impossible for either the Red Air Force or the Luftwaffe to claim total air control during much of the War. Instead, the combatants concentrated their forces in support of the great land battles—along the Polish frontier at the start of the War, later at Moscow, then Stalingrad, the Crimea and Kursk, and finally at Berlin, where 7,500 Red Air Force planes literally darkened the skies over the German capital.

destroyed—322 by flak and enemy fighters, 1,489 on the ground. The Luftwaffe had lost only 35 aircraft—several to their own SD-2 fragmentation bombs, dubbed "Devil's eggs," which had a nasty habit of getting stuck in their magazines and, at the slightest shock, blowing up the plane that carried them.

For days, then weeks, the slaughter continued unabated. Not even the Luftwaffe's grandiose Reich Marshal Hermann Göring could believe the German claim that 2,500 Soviet planes had been destroyed through June 24. Göring ordered a recount—only to learn that the original number had fallen short by 200 to 300. Assuming that the Soviet Air Force had ceased to exist as a threat to German air superiority, the Luftwaffe soon diverted its energies from assaults against airfields and began to concentrate almost exclusively on providing close support for the onrushing panzer columns.

But the Germans had underestimated. Whatever else it lacked, the Red Air Force was abundant in its numbers, and many Russian bombers had been based in the Soviet interior, which was as yet untouched by the enemy. Now, striving to gain time by slowing the diverging Wehrmacht drives toward Moscow in the center, Leningrad in the north and Kiev in the south, Stalin showed no qualms in sacrificing hundreds of bombers.

The Russians' clumsy tactics astounded and sometimes even appalled their opponents. Almost invariably, the Soviet SB-2s and DB-3s continued to attack in broad daylight and without fighter escort. Eschewing any attempt at evasive action, they clung stubbornly to a tight wedge formation that made them easy prey. During the first sorties, they dropped their bombs from 10,000 feet, as prescribed by prewar regulations. When that proved ineffective, they began making their runs at 3,000 feet or less—and were met by murderous fire from antiaircraft gunners.

A Russian bombing sortie near Kiev was typical in its execution—and its fate. As a German officer described it, "Ten Soviet bombers flew steadfastly toward their target. German fighter pilots were leisurely picking them off, while the formation of bombers seemed to make no effort to evade the attack. Faithfully holding their formation and following their leader, the Russian bombers continued onward until all of them were destroyed."

Moreover, German fighter pilots quickly discovered that, thanks to the Soviet fetish for secrecy, only the leaders of the bombing flights were thoroughly briefed as to the mission—or were even provided with maps. Therefore, if the Luftwaffe could knock out the leader of a Red bombing formation, the other aircraft would not know what else to do but abandon the mission and head for home.

Soviet fighter tactics were equally ineffective. At the first sign of the enemy, the Russians would hurriedly gather in a defensive circle, each pilot depending on the plane behind him for covering fire. There was, however, a major flaw in this merry-go-round formation. Recalled one Luftwaffe veteran: "If German fighters succeeded in breaking up the defensive circle, most of the Soviet pilots were then helpless." In many dogfights, the Soviets never got a chance to form their circle, but were caught by surprise from behind. As Luftwaffe Major Gerhard Barkhorn explained, many Russian fliers "were never taught to clear their tails. They never looked around in the cockpit and it was relatively easy to approach a flight of them and score several kills before they knew what was happening." Barkhorn knew what he was talking about: Before the War was over, he would shoot down an astronomical 301 enemy planes.

Small wonder, then, that these were glory days for the Luftwaffe. In the Minsk area, Fighter Wing 51 knocked down 114 Soviet planes on June 30 alone. Over the Dvina River, where Soviet bombers were trying to blunt the Wehrmacht thrust toward Leningrad, Messerschmitt 109Fs of the Green Heart Wing shot down 65 in a single day; the unit's

Major Emil Lang accounted for 18—and for an extraordinary 72 during a three-week period.

Still, as they had from the start, the Luftwaffe pilots found cause for sober consideration in their opponents' behavior. Sometimes the Russians seemed craven beyond comprehension. High-flying German pilots, for example, frequently looked down and saw, several thousand feet beneath them, Soviet interceptors simulating fierce combat maneuvers and firing their guns furiously into empty airspace. "This curious action," wrote a Luftwaffe officer, "was later explained by Russian prisoners, who testified that the commissar had ordered all Soviet fighters to take off and to engage the enemy in combat until he had left the target area. Because of their short flight durations, German fighters had to return to their bases within 15 minutes, in any case, allowing Soviet fighter units to report that they had 'driven off the attackers.'"

On the other hand, many Russians fought with a raw valor that could hardly have been inspired only by fear of their political officers. The deliberate ramming, called *taran* and generally undertaken only after ammunition had been exhausted, not only continued but was developed into more or less formal techniques that gave the Soviet pilots at least an outside chance for survival.

A favored method required that the Russian fighter pilot overtake a slower Luftwaffe bomber from the rear, cut back his speed so that he was flying only infinitesimally faster than the German and flick his propeller into the control surfaces of the enemy plane. "This can be judged to a nicety," explained Lieutenant Victor Kiselev after a successful ramming. "You only want to touch him very slightly with the tip of your screw."

Obviously, such a sophisticated form of *taran* required a delicacy of touch possessed by few Soviet airmen, especially at that stage of the War. For those of lesser skills, there remained the all but suicidal expedient of simply smashing into the enemy. At least that ensured a one-to-one loss ratio. In conventional dogfights and air-to-ground actions, the increasingly aggressive Soviets were nevertheless forced to endure losses of five or more aircraft for *every* German plane demolished. Including the first calamitous surprise attacks, the Luftwaffe claimed the destruction of 7,500 Soviet planes during the first month—which was probably not too far wrong. At the same time, the Germans admitted to 774 of their own aircraft lost.

In numerical terms, then, the Luftwaffe held an overwhelming attritional advantage of about 10 to 1. But percentile statistics presented a far less rosy picture: While the Soviets had lost nearly 70 per cent of the air force with which they had begun the War, the Germans had suffered the destruction of almost 60 per cent of the planes originally available to them on the Eastern Front. In comparative terms, the Luftwaffe's strength was being drained to a degree that alarmed its commanders.

Moreover, the Soviet losses were mainly old and obsolete craft, while the German losses were modern Me 109s, Ju 88s and He 111s. Worse, even in these early stages of the War, Soviet aircraft replacements—in the form of new models—were coming in at a rate far faster than the Luftwaffe could match. German industry, which had also to provide planes for the western war against Great Britain, could not serve the needs of both fronts.

The new Soviet planes *(pages 128-139)* were of course an absolute necessity for the survival of the Red Air Force. Still, flung into action with pilots insufficiently trained in their use, and often employed in ways that their designers had never envisioned, they were by no means an unqualified success.

The MiG-3 fighter, for example, was specifically intended by designers Artem Mikoyan and Mikhail Gurevich to offer its best performance as an interceptor at 19,000 feet and above. Given a power plant too big for its body, it was difficult to maneuver at lower altitudes—where the governing circumstances of the Soviet-German air war forced it to do most of its fighting.

But if many Russian pilots disliked the MiG-3, they loathed the LaGG-3, which had been designed by the team of Semyon Lavochkin, Vladimir Gorbunov and Mikhail I. Gudkov. With an airframe constructed of birch layers impregnated with plastic, the machine was decidedly overweight and, as a result, not only climbed slowly but displayed a lethal tendency to spin out of steep turns. In a play on its initials, fliers soon dubbed it the *Lakirovanny Garantirovanny Grob*— Varnished Guaranteed Coffin.

Altogether, 3,322 MiG-3s and 6,528 LaGG-3s would be delivered to the Red Air Force during their brief production lives, and some of them would remain in service until the end of the War. In the meantime, Soviet factories were ordered to concentrate on the most successful of the new fighters—the Yak-1.

Scarcely a decade before, Alexander Yakovlev had been a lowly mechanic at Moscow's Central Airfield. Now, at 33, he was known as a lover of speedy cars, fast women, strong spirits—and the sporty little airplanes he had designed during peacetime. Turning his ample energies to combat aircraft, he came up with a model whose graceful lines soon won it the nickname among factory workers of *Krasavchik*—or "Beauty."

It had its flaws: It performed poorly at high altitudes, and the murky Plexiglas of its cockpit canopy could scarcely be seen through. But as a low- to medium-altitude fighter it handled comfortably and could complete a 360-degree turn in 17 seconds. Its simple engine was durable and relatively easy to maintain even under the harshest field conditions. Its instrumentation was rudimentary, but to the Russians that was a virtue: As one Soviet air colonel dryly commented, there was no need to "distract" pilots with a lot of fancy gadgets.

Before the Yak-1 finally gave way to the advanced Yak-7, more than 8,700 planes would be produced—and Beauty would have done yeoman duty as the mainstay of the Soviet fighter force during its period of terrible crisis.

Among the last of the new aircraft to reach Soviet combat units was one of the crudest and clumsiest airplanes ever to find a place in the wartime inventory of a major power. Because of the irregularity of its profile, it was fondly known to its pilots as "the Hunchback"; to the Germans, it was *der Schwarze Tod*—or "the Black Death." And before it had been many weeks in service, Joseph Stalin would telegraph the factories engaged in its manufacture to command a speed-up in production, saying: "The front needs these aircraft like air or bread."

Sergei Ilyushin's Il-2 Shturmovik ground-attack plane was designed as nothing less than a flying tank, with more than 2,000 pounds of steel armor built in as an integral, stress-bearing part of its structure. The future Soviet Air Marshal Alexander Yefimov, who first flew a Shturmovik as a 19-year-old wingman in 1942, later wrote that the Il-2 had "a sort of monumental strength. In it, you felt protected against all dangers during operations under enemy fire."

Yefimov's first Shturmovik sortie came against German troop trains at Osuga Station, between Rzhev and Vyazma. "While we were still approaching Osuga Station, Hitler's antiaircraft batteries opened fire on us," Yefimov recalled. "The dull, gray puffs of bursts, which gradually formed a thick shroud, arose above and below our flight path. The ground-attack aircraft flew through this shroud as through a fog. It was as though the surface of the aircraft was covered by pockmarks. Some holes were large, the size of a fist, and others were smaller. But in spite of the numerous fragment hits, the engine was working normally and the aircraft was still responding."

During the Soviet attack, Yefimov became separated from the rest of his flight, which gave him "an unexpected tactical advantage. Either the enemy had lost sight of me or he thought I had been shot down. Be that as it may, I gained a relative freedom of action and again plastered the Hitlerite antiaircraft gunners with cannon and machine-gun fire. I belted them with short bursts and then immediately launched four rockets. They blew up right on the battery's location."

Yet neither Soviet men nor machines could stall the drive of the German ground forces. On July 16, Smolensk surrendered, and the way to Moscow lay open. It remained for none other than Adolf Hitler to grant respite to the Soviet capital: Over furious protests from most of his army commanders, he decided to consolidate his flanks. Ordering Bock's

Defending Moscow from German bombers in 1941, antiaircraft gunners dot the sky over Red Square with a barrage of exploding shells. The spires of the Kremlin are silhouetted by an enemy flare.

Army Group Center to halt, he dispatched General Heinz Guderian's panzer divisions southward to help complete the conquest of the Ukraine and sent General Wolfram von Richthofen's VIII Air Corps to the north to assist in the bombardment of Leningrad.

The Soviet Air Force had performed more effectively in the Ukraine than anywhere else, partly because the flat, open country offered little cover for ground forces, thereby enabling the Red airmen to inflict considerable damage. Beyond that, Russian fighter pilots were already entering a period marked by impressive tactical improvement—thanks to the growing influence of a 28-year-old senior lieutenant named Alexander Pokryshkin.

The son of a bricklayer, Pokryshkin had been flying for only four years, but by late summer of 1941 he had already demonstrated his brilliance as a pilot: Having downed his first Messerschmitt on the War's second day, he was by now on his way to becoming the Soviet Union's second leading ace, with 59 kills in the course of the War. But Pokryshkin was much more than a skilled sky driver: He was a close student of aerial combat who could—and did—impart what he had learned to his fellow pilots.

After each dogfight in which he participated, Pokryshkin later recalled, "I drew sketches of the various stages of aerobatics and made computations, trying to add on paper what I had done in the air." The walls of Pokryshkin's airdrome dugout were adorned with diagrams and charts, which he explained to other pilots, who gathered there during their off-hours.

Pokryshkin's unit, the crack 55th Fighter Air Regiment, had been among the first to reequip with the MiG-3. Unlike many other pilots, Pokryshkin liked the plane—and he used it as its designers had intended. "It is a sturdy machine," said Pokryshkin. "It behaves wonderfully at high altitudes, when its speed and maneuverability increase."

Pokryshkin took the MiG-3 up off the deck, where standard Soviet tactics had kept it. He and those who flew with him traveled an undulating course: "While on the whole sticking to one definite altitude, we maintained the necessary reserve of speed by a succession of small descents." From his position high in the sky, Pokryshkin could spot enemy formations at lower levels and calculate the most advantageous attack maneuvers, diving down to hit the enemy from the front, rear, flank or underbelly. Thus, Pokryshkin's tactical philosophy could be summed up in four words, which he was fond of repeating: "Altitude—Speed—Maneuver—Fire!"

In carrying out that credo, Pokryshkin helped bring about a basic reform of Soviet fighter tactics. "Before the War," he wrote later, "we were taught to fight in horizontal planes. Horizontal combat under modern conditions is, in the last analysis, a sort of 'rabbit tactics,' essentially tactics of defense, and passive defense at that." Instead, said Pokryshkin, "I decided the thing was to fight more boldly in the vertical plane."

A flight of new MiG-3s sweeps over the Moscow River on combat patrol in 1941. The Soviets assembled a force of nearly 600 fighters for the defense of Moscow; and though they suffered enormous losses, Red interceptors prevented the Luftwaffe from destroying the capital.

As other pilots followed his example in increasing measure, the rigid formations of the War's early days began to disappear. As testament to Pokryshkin's teaching talents, 30 pilots who flew under him would be named Heroes of the Soviet Union, between them scoring 500 kills during the War.

Yet during the dying days of that 1941 summer, not even the talents of Alexander Pokryshkin and his disciples could save the Ukraine—and neither could massive numbers. Since July, five Red Air Force divisions and two independent long-range bomber corps—more than 1,150 planes in all—had been thrown into the savage defense of Kiev. In September alone, the Soviets claim, they flew 10,000 missions against the Germans—but with results so disastrous that they remain utterly silent on the subject of scores. The net result was that the Soviet units defending the Ukraine were wiped out. On September 19, Kiev fell.

Nearly 800 miles north of the Ukraine, the Soviet situation was almost as dismal: The Wehrmacht's Army Group North stood on the threshold of Leningrad, Russia's second city. In a pathetic effort to keep the encircled city supplied, a little fleet of 30 twin-engined Li-2 transports (American DC-3s built under license) began operating an airlift while hungry citizens prepared to face the final German assault. It never came: Deciding to starve Leningrad rather than storm it, Hitler once more turned his attention toward the center. Operation *Typhoon,* the German drive on Moscow, was launched on September 30, with more than one million troops supported by 1,000 planes of Air Fleet 2.

In the air as well as on the ground, the Russians fought for the life of their capital. The VI Air Defense Fighter Corps, operating from airfields close to the city, comprised 34 regiments at various levels of strength, with another 29 on call from adjacent fronts if necessary. More than half of its 600 fighters were new models, and its pilots were among the best in the Soviet Union: For example, the 2nd Independent Night Fighter Squadron was made up entirely of veteran test pilots.

In anticipation of the German assault, the Soviet Air Force began flying against the Germans in mid-September, hitting the airfields from which the Luftwaffe planned to mount air raids on Moscow and the positions from which enemy ground troops would begin to roll. In the month's raids, the Soviets claimed to have destroyed 120 enemy aircraft on the ground and another 89 in combat along one front alone.

Nevertheless, Operation *Typhoon* opened as scheduled on September 30, and the German armies edged along the approaches to Moscow. By the end of the first week, amid some of the War's bitterest fighting yet, the Germans had taken the city of Bryansk, reached the outskirts of Tula and encircled a large contingent of Soviet troops at Vyazma. The trapped soldiers provided the Luftwaffe with static targets that had little or no air cover, and the prospects for Muscovites looked bleak indeed.

But the German armies had been delayed too long by Hitler's July orders. On the morning of October 7, Field Marshal von Bock at Smolensk noticed that the sky had turned gray and gloomy, and that a chill wind was cutting down from the north. That afternoon, rain began to fall, and by October 7 the entire front of Army Group Center was bogged down. The Russian *rasputitsa*—the "season of bad roads"—had started.

It lasted for more than a month. For day after sodden day, the drenching rain was broken only by periods of heavy fog, sleet and occasional snow, with sudden freezes quickly followed by thaws that only made matters worse. Bridges were ripped from their moorings by flooding streams, and the Russian roads—most of them mere dirt tracks in the best of weather—became bogs of mud as much as three feet deep. Tanks, transport trucks and troops alike became hopelessly mired, and a German commander despairingly wrote in his diary: "The boldest hopes are disappearing under rain and snow. Everything remains stuck in bottomless roads."

Now came the time for the Luftwaffe to pay the price for the heady successes of the summer months. Forever advancing its bases so as to stay close behind the armies it was committed to support, Air Fleet 2 was forced to use airfields of the crudest conceivable sort. Even at such cities as Minsk and Orel, the municipal airports taken over by German air units were little more than grass strips; elsewhere, the Luftwaffe tried to fly from wherever it could find reasonably level ground. Now, in the seemingly endless downpour, the airfields turned into patches of thick slime. And even when Luftwaffe pilots did manage to get into the air, the wretched weather frequently made visibility so poor that, in the words of a German officer, low-flying aircraft "ran the danger of colliding with trees on the many small hills of the region."

Conversely, as the Russian lines contracted, Soviet aircraft could operate from permanent bases with paved runways and adequate maintenance facilities guarding the capital at Vnukovo, Fili, Tushino, Khimki and Moscow Central itself. Even when required to use inferior fields, the Russians displayed a considerable talent for improvising. Shturmovik pilot Yefimov found that during the *rasputitsa* "mud clogged up the oil coolers during taxiing and takeoff, and because of this, the oil temperature increased sharply in flight.

"But our engineers and technicians found a way out. 'Take off with the oil coolers closed,' one of them advised our pilots, 'and open the ducts when you are airborne.' This is what we did and we made use of this simple procedure up to the end of the War."

However, for nearly a fortnight, the German armies struggled forward, advancing in places to within 50 miles of Moscow. And there they stayed, wallowing in a sea of mud and waiting for the *rasputitsa* to cease.

For the Red Air Force as well as for Moscow, the enemy's halt meant salvation at a moment of deepest crisis. Even as the German forces were nearing the capital's gates, Soviet aircraft production, which had sustained the Red Air Force in the first months of terrible attrition, suddenly plunged dramatically. From 2,329 planes in September the production rate fell dismally to about 800 in October and to fewer than 600 in November. The precipitous drop was the result of a migration of machinery and workers without parallel in history.

Only two days after the invasion of Russia, the Kremlin's leaders had established a special Evacuation Council to supervise the removal of industries in danger of being swallowed by the blitzkrieg. Before the colossal movement was done, more than 1,500 factories and 10 million workers and their families would be uprooted and transported 1,000 miles and more to the East—where lay rude refuge in the Ural Mountains, the Volga River region, Siberia and Central Asia.

Because much of the aircraft industry was concentrated around Moscow, its evacuation did not get fully under way until autumn, when the city was clearly menaced. Even then, there were those who shuddered at the immensity of the project. When Alexander Yakovlev told his fellow designer Nikolai Polikarpov of the plans to move aircraft plants, the veteran was aghast. "I know what it means to move," he said. "We evacuated the Russo-Baltic Railcar Factory from Riga to Petrograd during the First World War. Only 500 kilometers, but what a mess we made of it!"

Members of a Soviet air club parade past their PO-2 trainers. Planes like these were used to certify 24,000 prewar pilots.

Student pilots at a Soviet flying school serve as mechanics to familiarize themselves with the PO-2's five-cylinder engine.

ЗА СССР!

Soviet medics lift a wounded soldier into the improvised stretcher compartment of a ski-equipped PO-2 ambulance plane. Other PO-2s carried stretcher cases strapped to the lower wing on either side of the fuselage.

A PO-2 reconnaissance plane patrols the front near Moscow in 1942. Such planes were frequently unarmed; their only defense against German interceptors was to descend to treetop height and execute defensive maneuvers that often frustrated their faster but less agile pursuers.

The wood-and-fabric PO-2 was 24 feet long and had a wingspan of 37 feet. Powered by an air-cooled 110-hp engine, it could carry a payload of more than 500 pounds and fly 280 miles at a ceiling of 5,000 feet.

The many roles of the "duty sergeant"

Of all the aircraft utilized by the Soviet Air Force in World War II, the oldest, slowest—and most widely useful—was the dumpy little PO-2. A highly maneuverable biplane with a top speed of 81 mph, the PO-2 was designed by Nikolai Polikarpov in 1927 as an inexpensive, easy-to-fly basic trainer.

Serving in new roles during the War, the versatile PO-2 performed splendidly as a scout plane, artillery spotter, courier, transport, target tow and ambulance. As a night bomber, it was flown from improvised frontline strips by daring pilots, many of them women (pages 119-121), for low-level raids on German troop concentrations. So annoying were the nightly visitors that the Germans coined a sardonic nickname: "duty sergeants."

All told, Soviet factories turned out more than 40,000 PO-2s before production ended. It was a record for any aircraft type, and many of the planes survived the War to become crop dusters, forest-fire fighters or air taxis.

Polikarpov's fears were more than justified as entire factories were frantically dismantled and loaded—along with the workers who would eventually use them—onto railroad cars. Yakovlev, a bureaucrat as well as a designer, painted a rosy picture of the departing workers. Inspecting a boxcar, he "found double-tiered bunks with mattresses and rugs, an iron stove in the middle of the floor, a table and chairs, a kerosene lamp swinging from the ceiling, and inquisitive and cheerful children's faces peeking from the bunks." He was especially pleased when told that the train included a dining car.

The facts were more melancholy. As many as 50 people were herded into boxcars too small for half that number. "At night," recalled one worker, "it was so crowded people took turns sleeping, often atop one another." Choking on the sour smoke that billowed from unvented wood-burning stoves, relieving themselves through holes chopped in the floors of the freight cars, subsisting on the thin rations passed out to them at way stations, the workers made their long, miserable way to the unknown and unimagined regions that awaited them. And when winter fell while they were in transit, uncounted thousands froze to death or were maimed by frostbite.

But millions lived to reach such settlements as Sverdlovsk, Magnitogorsk, Komsomolsk and Novosibirsk, where a warren of wooden shanties, barracks, dugouts and tents to shelter 300,000 workers sprang up in 75 days.

On arriving, they found local residents already at work, frequently under killing conditions. "The earth was like stone," said one Sverdlovsk citizen, "frozen hard by our fierce Siberian frost. Axes and pickaxes could not break the stony soil. In the light of arc lamps, people hacked at the earth all night. They blew up the stones and the frozen earth, and they laid the foundations. Their feet and hands were swollen with frostbite, but they did not leave work. Over the charts and blueprints laid out on packing cases, the blizzard was raging."

Ordered to oversee operations at the Siberian town of Novosibirsk, Alexander Yakovlev left Moscow in style—in a Pontiac—but when the road petered out he was forced to complete his journey by train and then plane. Finally arriving at his distant destination, he found a factory already working—barely.

"There were several dozen planes in various stages of completion," he wrote, "every one of them lacking either ailerons or machine guns or oil radiators or radiator tubes or some other instruments or parts. Not a single one of them could be delivered."

Unfinished planes were moved to the factory airfield to wait until the missing parts could somehow be supplied. As the Siberian winter set in, "this crazy accumulation of planes was soon buried under several feet of snow. The airfield came to look like a graveyard. Only the noses and tails of planes could be seen sticking out above the blanket of snow."

Nevertheless, under Yakovlev's driving hand, the necessary parts were found—or made on the spot. The plant produced its first operative Yak-1 three weeks after his arrival. The buried planes were dug out and made flyable. Production rose steadily—until, 11 months later, the factory would put out seven and a half times as many aircraft as it had during its best Moscow days. Similarly, in Saratov, where an assembly line began production before walls or a roof had even been built, the first MiG-3 took to the air after only 14 days.

Yet not even the most fantastic effort could prevent the production slump caused by the massive industrial dislocation—or get new planes to Moscow when the city needed them most.

Within the capital city, Muscovites had been bracing for the onslaught ever since July. They had turned subway stations into air-raid shelters, enlisted civilians to walk anti-incendiary patrols and camouflaged all the important buildings. The walls of the Kremlin were painted to resemble a row of houses, Lenin's tomb in Red Square was covered with sandbags and made to look like a village house, and the golden domes of the Kremlin churches were boarded over with dark timber. Now, while the German armies on the city's outskirts waited for the weather to change, some 450,000 Muscovites labored at digging trenches and tank traps around the city. Antiaircraft defenses had been built up to 800 guns, and the gunners had become practiced at repelling German nuisance raids. Air Force pilots marched past their regimental colors, then knelt to deliver a solemn oath: "I swear to you my country and to you my native Moscow that I will fight relentlessly and destroy the Fascists."

In the desperate days of the summer, Moscow was all but defenseless; one of its fronts was down to a mere 106 operational fighters and 63 bombers. By reducing less imperiled areas to threadbare strength, Stalin managed by September 30 to assemble a total of 936 planes for the defense of Moscow.

By early November it was clear that the Japanese had turned their baleful gaze away from the Soviet Union and toward the Pacific. Stalin was therefore able to summon another 200-odd planes from the Far East, bringing the overall air strength at Moscow to 1,138 planes. Some of the new reinforcements had already arrived when, on November 15, Wehrmacht wheels and tank treads began to roll over firmly frozen ground in a renewal of the assault on Moscow.

In cold weather and beneath a pale sun, the Wehrmacht pushed toward Moscow by brute strength. But not for long. After a few days, and earlier than usual, the sky grew gloomy, temperatures dived below zero and snow began to fall—and fall and fall. The Russian winter, which had been Napoleon's nemesis and would yet be Hitler's, had arrived.

Having counted from the outset on another blitzkrieg victory, the German forces were singularly unprepared. The Luftwaffe, which had no freeze-resisting lubricant, no engine-warming devices, no established cold-weather procedures, began to suffer almost immediately. Aircraft engines refused to start, rubber tires became brittle and unsafe, and tools had to be heated before ground crews could use them.

Near their advanced bases, German airmen took shelter in peasant huts, in farm outbuildings, in abandoned schools and post offices. They got to their airfields on makeshift snowplows—captured ammunition carriers to which spade-shaped iron wedges had been fastened. Some units were marooned for weeks at a time while snow drifted to heights of 20 to 30 feet over their planes.

The Red Air Force was by no means immune to winter's cruelties. But, as a German officer noted, the Soviets "were accustomed to these conditions and were better able to cope with them than the German fighters, who were experiencing their first Russian winter."

As they had during the *rasputitsa,* the Russians took full advantage of their permanent bases and maintenance shops. Moreover, 30 airfield service battalions and nine engineer battalions were formed, and mobile aviation workshops were transported by rail to wherever they were most needed. To keep the planes flying, Soviet ground crews

In a dramatic ceremony, an air regiment, newly honored with a Guards designation, kneels in front of its Il-4 bombers to pledge fealty to Stalin.

rigged trucks with shafts that fit onto airplane propellers and worked as cranks to start balky engines; it was a technique the mechanics had employed during the Spanish Civil War, and it worked perfectly well in the Russian winter.

Their resourcefulness, combined with a primordial instinct for self-preservation, kept the Russians going. They mounted raid after raid against the hated Germans; for the three-week period of November 15 to December 5, by their own accounts, they flew 15,840 sorties versus a meager 3,500 for the Luftwaffe, and claimed a score of 1,400 German aircraft destroyed.

By December 5, advanced Wehrmacht units arrived within sight of Moscow's spires, only 10 miles away, and could continue no farther. It was the closest Hitler's legions would ever get to the Russian capital. The next day, the Soviets began a counteroffensive.

Itself on the edge of exhaustion, the Red Air Force played no major part in the counteroffensive. But it had already done more than anyone who had witnessed the War's first awful weeks might reasonably have expected: It had lived to fight another day.

Rescuing the factories

"It is as if the principal factories of New England were suddenly picked up, lock, stock and barrel and shifted bodily to the slopes of the Rocky Mountains." So wrote an American war correspondent of an incredible wartime feat—the mass evacuation in late 1941 of a major portion of Soviet heavy industry to save it from the Germans. In all, 1,523 plants, including hundreds of vital aircraft and engine facilities, were transported many hundreds of miles eastward to safety across the Ural Mountains. And with them went a human migration of 10 million workers.

The aircraft plants, mostly clustered around Moscow and Leningrad, kept producing under German fire until the last possible moment; then the machinery was frantically loaded onto trains and trucks and sent east over roads and tracks already clogged with military traffic and endless streams of refugees. The journey took anywhere from two weeks to a month, often in freezing rain and bitter cold, and uncounted thousands of workers perished in their packed, poorly ventilated boxcars.

At the destinations, all was chaos. Small industrial towns were overwhelmed by the influx. In one instance, four aircraft plants arrived more or less simultaneously at a site intended for one; a level-headed manager combined them into a single giant complex, with some production lines operating in the open until shelters could be built. The workers, many of them women and teenagers, often lived beside their machines in crude wooden huts, subsisting on bread and a thin soup made from beet greens.

There were monumental shortages of tools and materials—to say nothing of skills. Wood replaced aluminum for some aircraft components, and the parts had to be shaped by hand; craftmanship and fine tolerances were forgotten in the rush to produce. And produce the workers did. Laboring around the clock in 12-hour shifts, the inspired assembly brigades often rolled out their first plane from a roofless new plant scarcely two weeks after arrival. The factories making Yak fighters and Shturmovik ground-attack planes met Stalin's demand for three planes a day in less than three months. By the end of 1942, only a year after resuming production, the new plants were churning out warplanes at the record rate of 2,000 a month.

Truck convoys and trains are hastily loaded with equipment and fuselages from a bomb-damaged but still-functioning plant in the path of the German advance. Some factories were stripped completely within five days of receiving the order to evacuate.

At a pass in the Ural Mountains, 800 miles from Moscow, trucks loaded with partly finished wing sections churn through thick mud, while a train carrying machinery and half-completed planes labors along an elevated roadbed. Truck convoys usually broke camp long before dawn, when the mud was frozen and offered better traction.

While machinists stamp out aircraft parts on presses connected to portable generators outside an unfinished Urals plant, other recently arrived workers prepare a meager meal and nail together temporary shelters. Production has already begun on the roofless factory's floor, and the first two Yak fighters sweep overhead on their way to the front.

4
Armies of the air

It was a sorry little town, lost in the swamps and forests to the south of Lake Ilman, midway between Moscow and Leningrad. Yet during the winter and spring of 1942, German propagandists would glorify it as "Fortress Demyansk"—and months after it had been left in the War's backwash, it would assume a significance never envisioned by the men who fought there or by the leaders who directed their destinies.

During the winter counteroffensive, Soviet ground forces had pushed the Germans back along a broad front. But Adolf Hitler, for reasons known only to himself, was determined to hang on to Demyansk as a springboard for future operations. It was a wildly illogical decision: The town possessed no rail connections, and as one Wehrmacht commander noted, "its roads were so bad that it would have been an impossible choice as assembly point for an army."

Left far in advance of the contracting German lines, about 100,000 men belonging to Army Corps X and II were surrounded by Soviet forces, which had linked up after swinging around Demyansk from the north and south. Now, thanks to Hitler's obduracy, the encircled troops must either perish or trudge into captivity—unless they could be supplied by air on a scale without precedent.

Ordered on February 18 to undertake a massive airlift, Colonel Fritz Morzik, chief of air transport for Air Fleet 1, was dubious about the mission's chances. "To ferry a daily quota of 300 tons to Demyansk," he told the air fleet's commander, "I need a standing force of 150 serviceable transports, and we have only half that number. To double it, you will have to draw on other fronts and drain the homeland of all available machines."

No matter. By the next day, scores of three-engined Ju 52 transports were forgathering at airfields within range of Demyansk, and Morzik had established a headquarters at Pleskau-South, a field about 150 miles from the Demyansk pocket. The day after, on February 20, the first transports touched down at Demyansk's tiny 800-by-50-yard airstrip.

In the beginning, the Ju 52s flew in pairs and hugged the ground, hoping to escape the attention of Soviet fighter patrols. Soon, however,

A formation of ground-attack Il-2 Shturmoviks sweeps low across the Russian steppes toward a target. At Stalingrad in January 1943, seven Shturmoviks destroyed 72 parked planes on a German airfield.

they found themselves falling victim not only to hedgehopping Red Air Force fighters, but also to enemy antiaircraft guns and Russian troops who blazed away with all the small arms they owned—including even flare pistols. One Ju 52 crashed after its pilot was wounded by a torrent of submachine-gun fire. After that, Morzik dispatched his planes in groups of 30 to 40, flying in tight formations above 6,000 feet and protected by swarms of fighters.

Day after day and week after week the Ju 52s kept coming—despite temperatures that sometimes fell to −40° F., despite thick clouds that frequently clung to the ground and despite the Red Air Force. As the aerial battle developed, Soviet fighters learned to wait until the escorting Me 109s were at the limit of their range and turning for home; then the Red pilots would slash down to attack the transports from the rear as they attempted to land at Demyansk or at Peski, an even smaller airstrip that the Germans had constructed within the pocket. Scores of Ju 52s were destroyed in this fashion, and by May the Luftwaffe had lost 265 aircraft to the Soviets.

The attrition rate was terrible, perhaps one third of all the aircraft committed at Demyansk, and it did nothing to redress the growing numerical imbalance between the Luftwaffe and the Soviets. But the results were deemed worth the cost. In 13 weeks, the Luftwaffe had

A bundled-up flight crew tramps to its Pe-2 bomber on a bitter winter morning in 1942. Using tricks learned in decades of Arctic flying—such as draining fuel and oil overnight and warming engines with nose hangars— Soviet ground crews could ready planes for action in temperatures as low as −40° F.

Huge highway-type rollers level and compact the snow on a Soviet airfield, permitting quick use by aircraft. Such equipment gave the Russians a tremendous advantage over the Luftwaffe, whose planes were often grounded for days when storms hit their improvised fields.

flown in 24,303 tons of weapons, ammunition, food and other matériel, plus five million gallons of gasoline; in addition, 22,093 casualties had been evacuated and 15,446 replacements brought into the pocket.

By May 18, the Germans had broken out of the encirclement—and the Demyansk airlift thereafter wound down. Far from rejoicing at the success of his effort, Fritz Morzik later lamented: "From this time on, German military leaders were inclined to be indiscriminately enthusiastic regarding airlift employment."

As for the Soviet Air Force, it had learned some crucial lessons at Demyansk that within six months would be applied with deadly effect near a great city on the Volga River.

During much of the year that began at Demyansk, the Red Air Force would continue to suffer adversity, especially in the Crimea and the Ukraine. But even while still in its slough, it would slowly and painfully reshape itself with reforms in organization, increasingly improved tactics and aircraft, and careful husbandry of its mounting resources. These were hardly the stuff of melodramatic headlines—yet at the hour of truth they would bring victory in one of history's epochal battles.

The changes began at the Air Force top—a perilous place to be.

The Soviet Air Force had known eight commanders since its establishment in 1918. Two, a dismissed commander and his successor, had been killed in the same air crash. Two others had been shot during the 1938 purges, and three more were executed, one after another, in 1941, when Stalin took lethal reprisal for what he deemed poor wartime performance. Much more fortunate was General Pavel F. Zhigarev, the Air Force commander at the time of Demyansk. In April 1942—perhaps partly because of the air arm's inability to halt the Luftwaffe in that campaign—he was shipped off to remote duty in the Far East.

His successor was General Alexander Novikov, who would preside over the Soviet Air Force for the War's duration. Now 41, Novikov had followed a well-traveled path to his new eminence. He joined the Communist Party in 1920, attended the Frunze Military Academy (the Soviet equivalent of West Point) and, after a stint as an infantry officer, was assigned to aviation. Although he passed his pilot's examination, Novikov was primarily a desk man, not a flier. As such, he was air commander of the Leningrad Military District at the War's onset.

In the disastrous days following June 22, 1941, Novikov displayed admirable energy. Patching together the fragments of his own air units and what remained of the Baltic Military District and Navy air arms, he sent out the planes in a forlorn attempt to slow the German drive. Losses were high and successes were few, but the effort doubtless saved Novikov's life: Among his fellow regional air commanders, the Western District's General I. I. Kopets frustrated an NKVD firing squad by committing suicide, the Baltic District's General A. P. Ionov simply vanished, and the Kiev District's General E. S. Ptukhin was arrested and, months later, executed. (While in prison, Ptukhin expressed his feelings about Stalin. "If I had known," he said, "I would have first bombed our Dear Father, and then gone off to prison.")

Novikov's personality was elusive. "He was a dedicated, honest and honorable man," wrote Nikita Khrushchev, who knew him well during the War years. Then Khrushchev added: "He drank more than was probably good for him." But whatever else he may or may not have been, Novikov was a demon for hard work—and within a month after assuming command he had initiated institutional reforms that would provide a basis for the resurgence of the Soviet Air Force.

During the pre-Novikov period, as one Soviet analyst put it, the "scattering of aviation had resulted in strikes being made everywhere, but they have all been weak ones." Novikov's job was to create greater concentration of power, and to that end a directive was issued on May 8, 1942: "In the interest of increasing the striking force and successfully employing mass air strikes it is ordered to combine the air forces of the western front into a unified air army, giving it the designation of the First Air Army."

As the forerunner of air armies yet to come, the First was given two fighter and two composite divisions, a PO-2 night bomber regiment, a reconnaissance squadron and a liaison squadron. All told, there were fewer than 300 aircraft, a meager force indeed when compared with the mighty fleets of more than 1,000 planes apiece that would equip 17 air armies by War's end.

To ensure close coordination, each newly organized air army was assigned to support a specific ground army group, and the commanding officers of the air armies were made directly responsible to the army group commanders, under whom they served as deputies. This was the idea General Georgi K. Zhukov had pioneered in Manchuria; it was the reorganization under way on a casual basis when the Germans struck; but now it would become a Soviet Air Force religion. Moreover, to achieve greater flexibility, Novikov moved to create strong reserves that could rush to assist the air armies wherever the fighting was heaviest. When Novikov took over, the Soviets had only 10 reserve groups of

about 100 planes apiece; before he was done, reserve corps made up more than 40 per cent of the entire Red Air Force.

What was more, the lessons of fighter ace Alexander Pokryshkin and other successful pilots were being disseminated throughout the Air Force. Fighter pilots were taught to use sun and cloud cover, to fight on the dive, to hold their fire until they could direct short, well-placed bursts at close range, to stay together and fight as a team. All of this might have seemed too obvious for words—except that most of the experienced Soviet pilots were dead, that the replacement pilots were raw graduates and that in any case their training had heretofore been brief and lax. Yet another element was added: Pilots who broke off from dogfights without orders or who abandoned the bombers they were supposed to be escorting were disciplined by the political commissars. Unit commanders were told they would be expected to fly on combat missions, both to set an example and to keep an eye on the performance of new pilots.

The air armies, the reserves and the improvements in training were long strides in the right direction—but they came too late to save the Crimean citadel of Sevastopol.

For the Germans' spring offensive, Field Marshal Erich von Manstein's Eleventh Army was assigned to clear the Russians out of their foothold on the Kerch Peninsula in the eastern Crimea, then storm Sevastopol, which had been sealed off by land since mid-November 1941. With a certain grim whimsy, Manstein named his project Operation *Trappanjagd*—Bustard Hunt.

The operation began on May 8, and the Luftwaffe easily seized complete air superiority. The Soviet High Command, convinced that the main German thrust would be directed against Moscow, had retained its strongest air units in that sector, leaving the Crimea with a feeble force.

In the event, most of the Soviet air units in the Crimea cleared out for the Caucasus so hastily that 300 aircraft were left abandoned on their fields to be captured at the enemy's leisure. A pathetic handful of about 60 fighters and bombers was withdrawn to Sevastopol's environs to defend the doomed city.

They were no hindrance to the 723 Luftwaffe bombers that appeared over Sevastopol in the final stages of the offensive on June 2. For five days, the Luftwaffe's VIII Air Corps smashed Sevastopol with 2,264 tons of high explosives and 23,800 incendiary bombs. Then, on June 7, German artillery opened fire and infantry moved toward the maelstrom.

Sevastopol's minuscule air complement was utterly unable to strike at the enemy. So close were the German lines to the city's only airfield that observers could see clouds of dust rising whenever Soviet planes revved their motors for takeoff; within 30 seconds, the field was plastered by artillery fire, and Luftwaffe fighters picked off the few planes that managed to get off the ground. The Soviets attempted a night resupply operation with transports running the gantlet of German flak and fighters. But it was only a pale shadow of the German effort at Demyansk

General Alexander Novikov, commander of the Soviet Air Force, consults a map with an aide at his Moscow headquarters. Novikov personally directed the air battle at Stalingrad in 1942, committing a third of his force, 1,400 planes, to the four air armies fighting for air superiority and supporting ground troops in the beleaguered city.

111

four months before. By July 1, when the defenses at Sevastopol finally crumbled, the Red Air Force had managed only 288 flights, many of which had ended in disaster. Overall, the Soviets lost 141 planes at Sevastopol. The Luftwaffe's VIII Corps, for all its furious activity, counted only 31 planes downed in combat. Once more the lessons of air power had been demonstrated to the Soviets.

Yet in spite of the smashing Luftwaffe success at Sevastopol, an ominous—for the Germans—pattern was beginning to emerge. All too clearly, the Luftwaffe could still assemble forces sufficient to seize and maintain superiority in the skies above enormous ground battles. But that capacity was becoming increasingly limited. And elsewhere—with the help of a relocated aircraft industry that by the spring of 1942 was producing approximately 1,400 planes a month—the Soviet Air Force was gaining experience and achieving an

A crane hoists a new Shturmovik over a crowded production line relocated beyond the reach of German bombers in 1942. The banner exhorts workers to sacrifice "Everything for victory, everything for the front."

efficiency well adapted to the harsh conditions under which it operated.

During the summer, a U.S. military team, headed by Major General Follett Bradley and visiting Russia in order to facilitate lend-lease shipments, was given a rare glimpse of the Red Air Force in the field. It was most enlightening.

Driving to a mile-square sod airfield on rough, slightly rolling ground about 40 miles west of Moscow, the Americans found it bordered by a heavy pine forest, which "hid all the equipment and personnel so that from the air or the ground the field was apparently deserted."

The Bradley team reported that "when one approached within 200 feet of the edge of the woods, the revetments concealing the bombers became vaguely visible. A square portion of the brush and trees had been cut out, leaving room in which to park an airplane." To protect the aircraft from flying bomb splinters, logs were piled 10 feet high on three sides of each little clearing. "The top of the walled-in space," said the report, "was covered by a camouflage net covered with garlands."

Based at the field was a squadron of Pe-2 light bombers, with 10 planes being readied to take off on a mission against a German-held railway yard and supply dump. The Americans were taken to the squadron "briefing room"—rough tables, benches and a bulletin board beneath a camouflage net within the forest. "Check points were announced," said the Bradley report, "and, since the weather at the objective was doubtful, a secondary objective was given. The bombing altitude was given as 4,000 meters, but the crews were advised that if the weather was unfavorable a minimum bombing altitude of 800 meters would be permitted."

"The take-offs were made individually," said the report, "and only ten minutes transpired between the time that the engines were started and the time that the last ship left the ground. The roughness of the field made each take-off appear hazardous. A run of about 2,500 feet was used before a heavily-laden ship got into the air, and it did not gain any altitude for another 2,500 feet."

Over the next two hours, the Bradley team listened to radio reports as the Soviet bombers met their fighter escorts, arrived over their primary target, dropped their bombs and saw fires beginning to blaze. Although several of the Russian planes were damaged by antiaircraft shrapnel, all returned safely to their base in the pine woods. Bradley and his men were impressed with the efficiency of the Soviet operation. Although the equipment was in some instances crude, the Russian pilots and crews appeared to have a high standard of proficiency. In his report Bradley commented that "every man knows his job thoroughly."

Bradley's assessment would be put to the ultimate test in the war by now exploding with apocalyptic fury 600 miles to the southeast.

On June 28, 1942, three German armies crashed out of their sectors and surged east and south toward Stalingrad, the mighty Volga River industrial center favored by the Soviet dictator. The capture of Stalin-

Scores of new Shturmoviks, awaiting delivery to combat units, line both sides of a factory airstrip behind the Urals in the summer of 1942.

grad was by no means a primary German purpose. Instead, the city was merely a place to be sealed off before the invading armies swung south toward the Caucasus—whose oil fields were the true objective of Adolf Hitler's 1942 summer campaign.

As the battle unfolded, two of the armies wheeled south to join in an attack on Rostov, the gateway to the Caucasus. The Sixth Army, under Lieutenant General Friedrich Paulus, would go it alone to the Volga.

To support the Sixth Army in its advance, the Luftwaffe—as in the past—had managed an impressive concentration of strength. Available to Air Fleet 4, commanded by General Wolfram von Richthofen, a cousin of the World War I ace, were 1,200 combat planes—about the same number with which Hitler had launched *Barbarossa*. Freed from the awful rigors of the Russian winter, the Luftwaffe was now operating at its full, fearsome efficiency.

Against this huge and finely honed assemblage stood the month-old Soviet Eighth Air Army under Lieutenant General Timofei T. Khryukin, who, although only 32, was already a veteran of the air wars in Spain and the Far East. Khryukin did the best he could with what little he had. As at Sevastopol, the High Command had decreed that the bulk of the Soviet Air Force be reserved for operations elsewhere: Stalin still believed that Moscow was the primary Wehrmacht objective. Khryukin's fledgling force possessed only 454 aircraft; and the men who flew them had not as yet absorbed the new doctrines and training imposed by Air Force chief Novikov. In scenes reminiscent of June 1941, Soviet bombers unaccountably flew in large formations to certain destruction. The fighter tactics of ace Alexander Pokryshkin were often ignored. Reconnaissance was virtually nonexistent as pilots lost their way; one flier in the 88th Fighter Regiment landed his plane beside a Russian column on the march to ask where he was. Shouts from the men that they were prisoners of war sent him running back to his plane under a fusillade from the German guards. Even with sizable reinforcements, losses were so great that by the beginning of October the strength of the battered Eighth Army was down to barely 188 planes, including only 24 fighters.

None other than Lieutenant General Vasili I. Chuikov, deputy commander of the Soviet Sixty-fourth Army, could testify about the extent to which the Luftwaffe commanded the skies. "Fighters and assault planes were constantly overhead," he later recalled. "They shuttled backward and forward flying east and back as calmly as if they were at home." Chuikov bitterly noted that on one particular day he did not see a single Soviet aircraft, while the enemy seemed to fill the skies: "We spent the whole day meandering about the steppe, being shot at and bombed."

Another memorable occasion very nearly cost Chuikov his life. While he was inspecting his front from the air, his PO-2 observation plane was attacked by a Ju 88. "A cat-and-mouse game began," Chuikov recalled. "It looked as though the enemy's cannon and machine-gun fire would cut our plane to pieces in the air. My pilot, taking his bearings from the sun, headed eastward, trying to find some small village behind which we could hide from the bird of prey pursuing us. But the steppe was bare," and after the Ju 88 made nine or 10 passes at the frantically dodging PO-2, "our plane struck the ground and split in two. As we were flying at ground level, the pilot and I were relatively unhurt." Chuikov emerged from the wreck with a bump on his forehead—and watched with vast relief as the German pilot, evidently assuming that the PO-2's passengers had been killed, flew away to the west.

From such harrowing personal experiences, Chuikov drew some broader lessons. "In modern warfare," he wrote, "victory is impossible without combined action by all types of forces and without good administration. The Germans had this kind of polished, coordinated action. A few minutes before a general attack, their aircraft would fly in, bomb and strafe the object under attack, pinning the defending troops to the ground, and then infantry and tanks with supporting artillery and mortar fire would cut into our military formations almost with impunity."

Before long, transferred and named commander of the Sixty-second Army within Stalingrad, Vasili Chuikov would put to good use the education he received in the field.

The city's time of travail was now at hand. At 4:30 a.m. on August 23, German tanks churned out of a bridgehead on the east side of the Don River and, with Stuka dive bombers paving the way, lanced straight for the Volga. Late that afternoon, leading panzer elements stood on the cliffs overlooking the river just north of Stalingrad. And then, from the west, came the steady drone of aircraft—hundreds of them.

In the largest Luftwaffe assault since June 22, 1941, Lieutenant General Martin Fiebig, who commanded VIII Air Corps under Richthofen, threw in everything he had. During the night of August 23-24, in wave after wave, 600 planes, including even Ju 52 transports converted to bombers, mounted 2,000 sorties. Far from having a strategic objective, the raid was designed to bring terror—more than half the bombs were incendiaries.

Russian survivors would later recall the night in kaleidoscopic, flame-filled snatches—a woman decapitated as she scurried along a sidewalk for safety, the screams of telephone operators buried in the debris of the exchange building that had collapsed upon them, rivers of blazing oil from ruptured tanks, the sight of lunatics, liberated from their bombed asylum, now wandering dazed and naked in one of the several gorges that intersect the city.

Watching the bombardment from a position near the Volga, a German soldier wrote: "The whole city is on fire. . . . That's what the Russians need, to stop them resisting." By next morning, more than 40,000 were dead.

Among the survivors was General Alexander Novikov, newly arrived to oversee the aerial defense of Stalingrad.

Novikov faced a fearful challenge. Stalin, previously preoccupied by

A German Me 109 fighter—one of 148 destroyed at Stalingrad—goes down in flames in this dramatic sequence of photographs recorded by the gun camera of a Soviet interceptor. The best Russian fighter pilots were assigned to roam the skies over Stalingrad as "free hunters," ready to pounce on any convenient target.

the possibility of a renewed German offensive against Moscow, had at last turned his attention to Stalingrad—and decreed that its defenders must fight to the last man. In response, Hitler, who had hitherto (and rightly) considered the city to be of slight strategic value, now declared that it must be seized at all cost. Thus, as much as it was a struggle of men and machines, the Battle of Stalingrad became a clash of dictatorial wills—and woe betide the commander who failed in his mission.

The ever-energetic Novikov went immediately to work. He called upon the brand-new, largely untrained and understrength Sixteenth and Seventeenth Air Armies to reinforce the decimated Eighth with 600 planes. He superintended airfield construction (25 operational and 19 decoy fields were eventually built for the Eighth Air Army alone), and he endlessly visited his units to lend moral support.

It made encouraging reading for the daily reports sent to Stalin. But in fact the Luftwaffe continued to rule the air—at least for the next few weeks. On September 3, for example, in an aerial attack coinciding with an all-out effort by Paulus and his Sixth Army to shove Stalingrad's ground defenders into the Volga, Ju 88s and He 111 bombers were able to operate in almost complete safety; scores of Me 109s kept the bomber lanes over Stalingrad clear of Soviet interceptors. "There was," wrote a Luftwaffe officer, "practically no evidence of Soviet air activity."

Still, the Soviets refused to surrender—and, for all their desperate plight, they were already preparing for the time when the tide of battle would turn in the air as well as on the ground. Determined not only to hoard his scanty frontline strength but to build a reserve for future offensive use, Novikov ordered his fighters to avoid full-scale melees. Instead, they adopted *zasada,* or ambush, tactics: Groups of fighters flying in pairs would hit small Luftwaffe formations, or pick off unescorted transports and reconnaissance planes. Another tactic was the "free hunt," in which fighters would roam the front attacking targets of opportunity in the air or on the ground. At the same time, borrowing a page from the German book, Novikov established forward observation stations, close behind the front lines at intervals of five or six miles, to provide radio guidance to Air Force fighters.

Among the early beneficiaries of the new system for control and response was a young Yak-1 pilot named Chumborev. On September 14, during a *zasada* patrol, Chumborev spotted an Fw 189 reconnaissance plane—easy prey for a Yak-1—spying on Soviet positions from about 3,500 feet. When Chumborev attacked, the German took cover in clouds. Chumborev followed, firing wildly—and often blindly.

From the ground, a Soviet radio post tracked the German plane as it nimbly dodged from cloud to cloud, giving Chumborev a running account of the enemy's movements. With such assistance, Chumborev finally caught the Focke-Wulf and rammed it from behind and below. Mortally damaged, the reconnaissance plane fluttered to the ground while Chumborev landed safely in a nearby field.

Despite such individual successes, the Luftwaffe continued to hold dominion—by day. The hours of darkness were a different matter. No sooner had the sun set than Soviet bombers rose from their well-camouflaged bases east of the Volga. Il-4 twin-engined night bombers of a newly formed long-range bomber force were dispatched to attack the German rear, while Il-2 Shturmoviks bored through the searchlights and flak to pound the Luftwaffe's forward airfields. But the mainstay of the night-bombing campaign was the old PO-2 biplane—trainer, observation plane and now bomb carrier.

Each flying as many as six sorties a night, their five-cylinder radial engines pop-pop-popping as they went (because of the distinctive sound, the Germans dubbed them *Nähmaschinen,* or ''sewing machines''), the awkward little planes attacked at timed intervals from different directions so as to confuse enemy gunners. By mid-October they had become such a nuisance that a German Sixth Army duty officer complained in a report: ''The untouchable nightly dominance of the Russians has increased beyond tolerance. The troops cannot rest, their strength is used to the hilt.''

Nothing, perhaps, in the saga of Stalingrad was more stirring than the fact that one of the most effective of the PO-2 units was the 588th Night Bomber Regiment—whose 400 members, from pilots and navigators to ground mechanics and armament fitters, were all women *(right)*.

The 588th was one of three women's air regiments. The others were the 586th Fighter Regiment, equipped with Yak-7Bs, and the 587th Bomber Regiment, which flew modern twin-engined Pe-2 light bombers. Sent to the Stalingrad area almost immediately after completing their flight training, the women had a number of problems, including one of simple muscular strength. Because of the Pe-2's stiff controls, the women of the 587th found it difficult to get the plane off the ground. Recalled one pilot: ''Most of us had to get our navigators to stand beside us on takeoff to help yank the stick back on a given command.''

For the women of the 588th Regiment in their pesky PO-2s, Stalingrad meant flying at night behind enemy lines in open cockpits, exposed to wind and rain, unarmed except for bombs and grenades, against a foe who soon took strong countermeasures. In their exasperation, the Germans formed special ''flak circuses'' composed of as many as two dozen 37-millimeter antiaircraft guns and supported by a searchlight platoon. Hidden by day, the lethal arrays were moved at nightfall into areas of expected Soviet attack; there, with guns and lights arranged in concentric circles, they awaited the coming of the *Nähmaschinen.*

To cope with the flak circuses, the women of the 588th devised a perilous technique. A pair of PO-2s would head for a target, where one PO-2 would distract German searchlights and gunnery while the other made its attack. The dangers and difficulties of the system were amply illustrated by the experience of Nadia Popova and Marina Chechnova, flying in tandem against a bridge at an important river crossing.

Their plan was for Popova to draw enemy fire while Chechnova attacked. Accordingly, Popova dived against the bridge at full throttle—

The White Rose and the Night Witches

Partly out of desperate need, partly out of a sense of Communist egalitarianism, the Soviet Air Force in World War II was the only major air arm to allow women to fly in combat units. Close to 1,000 women volunteers fought with courage and distinction in every sort of warplane, from Yak fighters to Shturmoviks.

Many of the women were integrated into regular Air Force units; the Soviets applauded Lilya Litvyak as the White Rose of Stalingrad, not so much for her blond, blue-eyed beauty as for her 12 victories as a member of a crack fighter unit. As early as 1942, three air regiments were composed entirely of wom-

en. The 586th Fighter Regiment was credited with 38 kills—17 by the top-scoring Olga Yamshchikova, a veteran instructor who volunteered for combat.

Some of the bravest women fliers belonged to the 588th Night Bomber Regiment. The Night Witches, as they were known, were equipped with slow PO-2 biplanes *(pages 94-95)*; nevertheless, in the course of the War they flew no fewer than 24,000 sorties over enemy lines, dropping 23,000 tons of bombs. Their casualties were high—and so were their honors. Of the 30 citations of Hero of the Soviet Union awarded Air Force women, 23 went to the Night Witches.

Fighter aces Lilya Litvyak (left) and Katya Budanova (center) scored a combined 22 kills before both perished in combat.

Major Yevdokia Bershanskaya (center), a prewar airline pilot and commander of the 588th Night Bomber Regiment, leads a group of Night Witches returning from a successful raid behind enemy lines.

Lieutenant Anna Yegorova piloted a Shturmovik throughout the War and was three times decorated for valor.

Lieutenant Valeria Khomyakova (second from right) tells fellow pilots of the all-woman 586th Fighter Regiment how she bagged a Ju 88 bomber in September 1942—the first German plane shot down by a woman.

Lieutenant Natalya Meklin joined the Night Witches as a 19-year-old pilot in 1942 and survived 840 missions in three years.

Rufina Gasheva (left) and Natalya Meklin display their decorations after each was made a Hero of the Soviet Union.

Home from a mission, Shturmovik gunner T. F. Konstantinova stands on the wing after securing her machine gun.

121

and noisily—and then, without bombing, took breakneck evasive action. "Wide, solid-looking beams of light were cutting through the sky from several directions, trying to trap me in one great pool of light," she recalled. "One of them swept right across the nose of my aircraft, but before he could track me back I had gone into a hard, diving turn and they lost me. The antiaircraft fire was intense. I could hear pieces of shrapnel tearing through the wings."

Meanwhile, Marina Chechnova had been waiting impatiently. "It wasn't a nice feeling," she said later, "knowing that your friend was inviting the enemy to shoot her down. They must have heard her very clearly, and I could see the flames from her exhaust pipes as she dived away from me."

Only after the Germans had begun their concentrated search for Popova did Chechnova swoop against the bridge, dropping several bombs that landed close to the target. Then the two pilots switched positions, with Chechnova as the decoy and Popova making the attack.

Later, Nadia Popova said tersely of their tactic: "It worked."

By the middle of October, with the ground armies locked like scorpions in deadly embrace, Stalingrad's toll had reached staggering proportions: The Germans admitted to 42,000 casualties; the Russians offered no figures, but lost at least as many men, and perhaps more. By early November, after a last spastic lunge, Paulus held 90 per cent of the ruins that had once been a city. But he had shot his bolt—and, as the temperature suddenly dipped to signal the onset of another Russian winter, the German bill for past mistakes fell due.

In his August thrust to the Volga, Paulus had done nothing more than blast open a hole in the Soviet lines along the Don, leaving his own lines of communication exposed to the large Russian forces that remained on his flanks. Since late September, when Stalin had approved plans for an eventual counteroffensive, the Soviet High Command had exercised consummate patience in building up its ground and air reserves at the expense of units actually engaged in fighting.

Now, with the scheduled moment of Russian retribution at hand, Novikov risked Stalin's wrath by asking for a brief delay: His aircraft numbers were adequate, but he was still painfully short of both fuel and ammunition. The surprisingly courteous reply from Moscow bore testimony to the importance attached to the Air Force role in the coming counteroffensive. In granting Novikov's request, the Soviet High Command said: "The experience of war indicates that we can achieve a victory over the Germans only if we gain air supremacy."

Finally, at dawn on November 19, the tempest broke, with more than a million Russian troops, 13,535 guns and 979 tanks pounding German positions. For its greatest effort to date, the Soviet Air Force had assembled 1,414 aircraft. And it had now achieved not only quantitative parity with the Luftwaffe but was catching up in quality as well. Virtually all of the fighters and fully 75 per cent of the entire force was of modern design, including the new La-5, a souped-up and much more effective version of the LaGG-3 fighter, and the Yak-9, a worthy descendant of the tried-and-true Yak-1. Late models of the already famed Il-2 Shturmovik were fitted with more powerful engines that enabled them to use shorter runways and gave them greater maneuverability; they now had a position for a rear gunner, which made the heavily armored attack plane even more difficult for the Luftwaffe to shoot down.

A weather front shut down most Luftwaffe air operations as the great Soviet counteroffensive got under way. During the next four days, only 150 sorties were flown in aid of the Wehrmacht's retreating Sixth Army. The German air commander, General Wolfram von Richthofen, wrote despairingly in his diary: "Rain, snow and ice-forming have completely prevented air operations and VIII Air Corps can direct only a few single aircraft to the attack. We must have good weather soon; otherwise there is no hope."

By stunning contrast, the Red Air Force mounted no fewer than 1,000 sorties during those same four days—almost all of them by the redoubtable Shturmoviks. Utterly heedless of death, the pilots simply took off and headed for the enemy—often at altitudes of 50 feet or less. And the white-camouflaged planes suddenly bringing death out of the white sky served as much as anything else to demoralize the already hard-pressed Germans.

The skies cleared on the 24th, and over the next seven days the three Soviet air armies at Stalingrad flew almost 6,000 combat missions against the reeling Germans. Roughly two thirds of the missions were now directed against German airfields. The Sixteenth Air Army alone claimed 63 enemy planes destroyed on the ground, with another 33 downed in aerial combat. Soviet losses were reported as 35 planes. Slowly, the Luftwaffe was being bled to death.

By then, the German High Command had made a fateful decision. It had been immediately evident that Paulus' Sixth Army could not withstand the massive Soviet ground and air assault. There were only two options: to make a fighting withdrawal or, rather than give up the ground earned at such bloody cost, to allow the Sixth Army to be surrounded and to have it cling grimly to Stalingrad until rescued. The answer should have been obvious—but visions of the airlift success at Demyansk still danced in some German heads. And from Hitler himself came the command for Paulus to stand fast.

The chief of VIII Air Corps, Martin Fiebig, first learned of the decree in a November 21 telephone conversation with the Sixth Army chief of staff, Major General Arthur Schmidt. Asked about Paulus' plans, Schmidt replied: "The C.-in-C. proposes to defend himself at Stalingrad." And how, asked Fiebig, did Paulus hope to keep his army supplied? Said Schmidt: "That will have to be done from the air." Fiebig was aghast. "A whole army?" he cried. "But it's quite impossible!"

To Fiebig and to most other experienced air commanders, overwhelming differences existed between Demyansk and the situation at

Stalingrad. With 250,000 men, the Sixth Army numbered two and a half times the force for which the Luftwaffe had strained itself to the utmost at Demyansk. The distances over which supplies would have to travel were vastly greater at Stalingrad than at Demyansk. And, not least, at Demyansk the airlift operators had been able, as Colonel Fritz Morzik said, "to look—and plan—toward the benign coming of spring," while at Stalingrad they faced only the horrors of another Russian winter. Most important of all, the Luftwaffe now confronted an entirely different opponent in the huge and increasingly well-trained and -equipped Red Air Force.

No sooner had Fiebig heard of the airlift plan than he called his own superior, General von Richthofen, who promptly protested to the Luftwaffe Chief of Staff, General Hans Jeschonnek. "You've got to stop it!" shouted Richthofen. "In the filthy weather we have here there's not a hope of supplying an army of 250,000 men from the air. It's stark, staring madness."

Jeschonnek, however, was helpless. After all, none other than Hermann Göring had grandly promised Hitler that "the Luftwaffe will supply the Sixth Army from the air."

On November 24, Richthofen's Air Fleet 4 received official orders to supply the Sixth Army with at least 300 tons of supplies daily. And on November 25, 1942, the airlift to Stalingrad began.

Memories of Demyansk had also lingered in Russian minds—and Soviet planners were determined not to repeat the mistakes of the earlier airlift battle. At Demyansk, Soviet fighters had merely hurled themselves at the strongly escorted fleets of Luftwaffe transports; there was no carefully thought-out and well-coordinated plan to seal off the air lanes to Demyansk. But there would be at Stalingrad.

To establish an air blockade of the pocket in which Paulus was snared, Novikov established four operational zones. The first, assigned to the bombers of the Seventeenth and part of the Eighth Air Armies, was beyond the periphery of the pocket and included the airfields from which the airlift transports must fly—initially Morozovskaya, 125 miles from Stalingrad, and Tatsinskaya, 155 miles away, and, later, Sal'sk, Novocherkassk and Rostov 60 to 80 miles farther away.

The second zone, divided into five sectors, was turned over to the fighters of the Sixteenth and Eighth Air Armies, along with the 102nd Air Defense Division, which were to patrol the corridors through which the German transports would fly to the Sixth Army pocket. A third zone, up to 19 miles deep, ringed the pocket with antiaircraft batteries along the air corridors. Finally, the fourth zone consisted of the five airfields within the 1,000-square-mile pocket, which were to be kept under relentless attack.

Those defenses—along with the weather—were effective from the start. During the first two days of the airlift, the Sixth Army received a total of only 130 tons of supplies. On the third day, almost nothing got

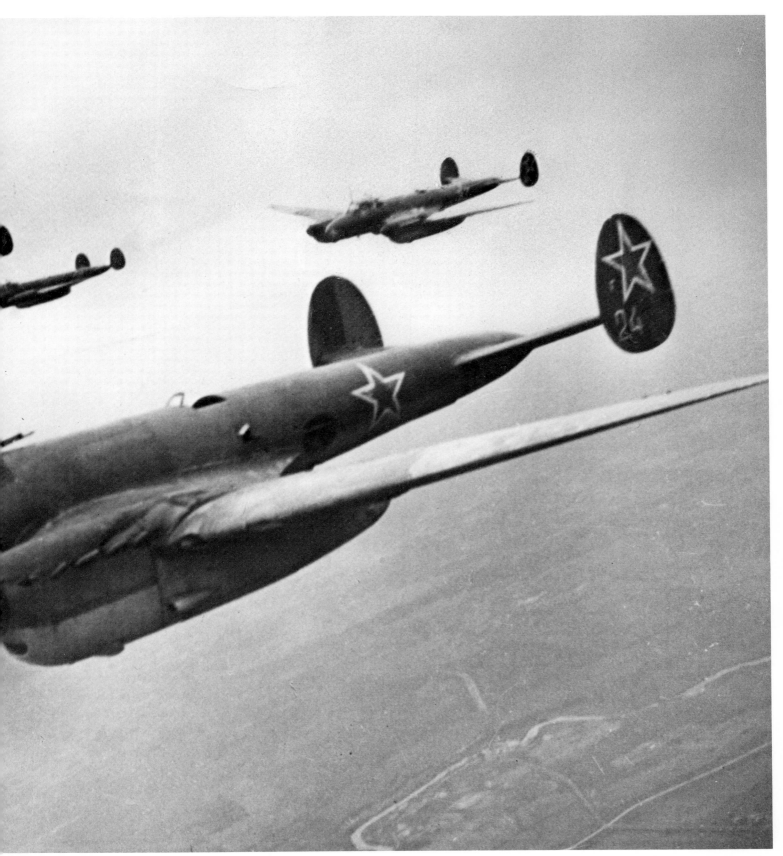

A flight of Pe-2 dive bombers heads for German positions near Leningrad in 1943. Pe-2 crews often flew three ground-support missions a day.

through, and General Fiebig wrote in his diary: "Weather atrocious. We are trying to fly, but it's impossible. One snowstorm succeeds another. Situation desperate."

In all but the worst weather, Soviet aircraft appeared in force, fighting with a skill and coordination the Luftwaffe had not previously encountered. On November 28, for example, three Yak-1s of the 287th Fighter Regiment shot down four Ju 52s. Two days later, planes of the 283rd Fighter Division intercepted 17 Ju 52s with an escort of four Me 109s; by the time the dogfight was done, five of the transports and one fighter had been destroyed. On December 2, another 17 German transports were demolished on the ground while unloading supplies within the pocket. And on December 11, eight La-5s and nine Yak-1s attacked 16 Ju 52s escorted by four Me 109s, scoring nine kills.

On that same day, General Fiebig flew into the pocket to confer with a disconsolate and reproachful Paulus, who had been receiving barely one sixth of the supplies the Sixth Army needed to survive. "With that," said Paulus, "my army can neither exist nor fight." It could hardly have helped that precious transport space was being taken up by thousands of trees that Hitler had ordered flown into the pocket to bring to the starving Sixth Army a bit of Christmas cheer.

The Luftwaffe responded to Paulus' pleas with a titanic effort. Even He 111 bombers were diverted to the airlift, their bomb bays crammed with 1,000 pounds of cargo apiece on each run. The shipments to Stalingrad inched upward to a peak of more than 280 tons on December 19. Then the pace was slowed by heavy fog—and grim events. On the evening of December 21, some 1,250 miles away at Hitler's Rastenburg headquarters in East Prussia, Field Marshal Albert Kesselring was witness to an extraordinary sight. Entering an office, he recalled, "I could see Göring sitting at his writing desk. He was sobbing aloud and time and again fell forward onto his desk."

Some time later, officers of the High Command explained to Kesselring that Göring had received very bad reports about Stalingrad. In fact, he had learned that Soviet troops had broken through the Italian Eighth Army on the Don and were now menacing the critical airlift bases of Morozovskaya and Tatsinskaya.

For Tazi, as Tatsinskaya was now known, the end came early on the morning of December 24. At 5:25 a.m., shells from approaching Soviet tanks began exploding on the airfield, instantly destroying a Ju 52. Although it was obviously time and past time for the German transports to clear out, Fiebig refused to order the evacuation without permission from higher authority. Five invaluable minutes were wasted while he tried to reach Richthofen over telephone lines that had gone dead. Finally, however, he gave in to the pleas of staff officers. "Right!" he said. "Permission to take off. Try to withdraw in the direction of Novocherkassk."

Total chaos ensued. With fog severely limiting visibility and with snow spraying from their passage, the big transports scrambled wildly in their

In the wake of a Soviet raid on a German supply field, burning Junkers 52 transports symbolize the failure of the Luftwaffe's ambitious airlift during the Battle of Stalingrad. The Germans lost so many transports that they were forced to convert some of their bombers into freight carriers.

frantic haste to escape. Two Ju 52s, lumbering from opposite directions, collided head on and exploded at midfield. Others got hopelessly tangled while taxiing and still others were smashed by Soviet shells. In all, 109 Ju 52s and 16 Ju 86s managed to get away—but they left behind them 60 wrecked transports.

Early in January, Morozovskaya followed its sister airfield into Soviet hands. From then on, although the Luftwaffe tried mightily to sustain the airlift from more distant bases, fewer and fewer transports got through the Red Air Force blockade. After New Year's Day, only twice did the blockade-runners deliver more than 200 tons in one day. And their losses were staggering. On January 9, Shturmoviks strafed and bombed the airfield at Sal'sk; of the 300 Luftwaffe planes parked on the field, 72 were destroyed. In the meantime, the Sixth Army was starving.

On February 2, radio contact with the Sixth Army was lost. That night, a German pilot flew over a snow-covered battlefield grown eerily silent. There were, he reported, no signs of continued fighting. In fact, Friedrich Paulus had surrendered, and the remnants of his army— more than 91,000 men—were already being marched into captivity.

The awful Battle of Stalingrad was over—at a cost to the Luftwaffe of 490 planes. The Soviets did not release their losses. But there could be no question: The saga of the Soviet Air Force as a formidable fighting machine was just beginning. ⌒

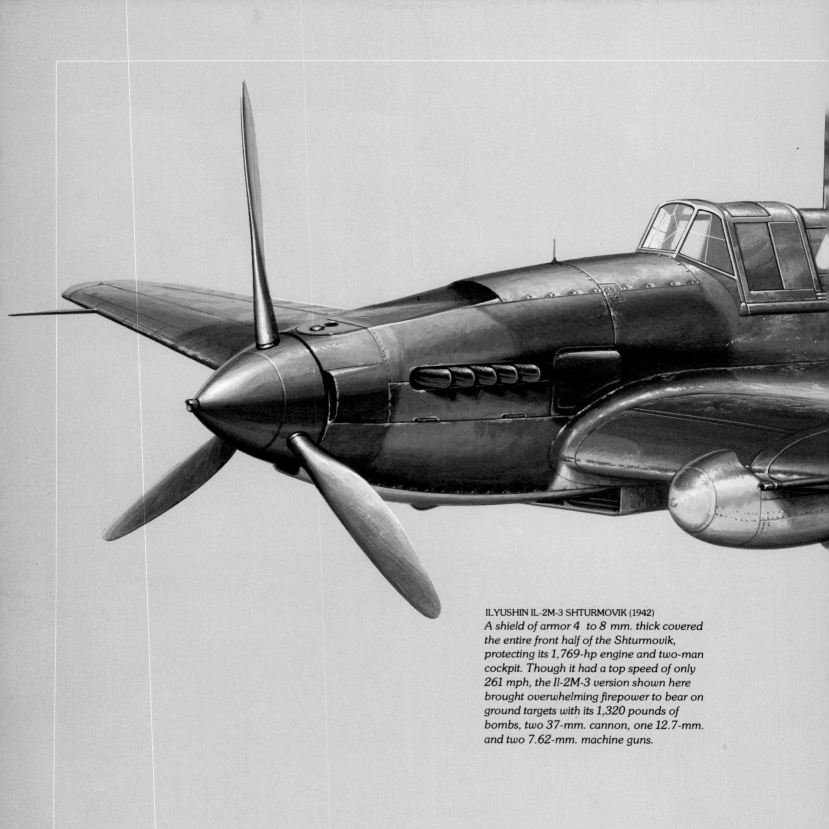

ILYUSHIN IL-2M-3 SHTURMOVIK (1942)
A shield of armor 4 to 8 mm. thick covered
the entire front half of the Shturmovik,
protecting its 1,769-hp engine and two-man
cockpit. Though it had a top speed of only
261 mph, the Il-2M-3 version shown here
brought overwhelming firepower to bear on
ground targets with its 1,320 pounds of
bombs, two 37-mm. cannon, one 12.7-mm.
and two 7.62-mm. machine guns.

A formidable arsenal of flying artillery

In the eyes of Soviet strategists, the Red Air Force was primarily an extension of the Army, a battlefield weapon whose purpose was to protect and pave the way for ground troops. Fighters were to clear the skies over the combat zone, while bombers were to be hurled against the enemy in massive barrages of flying artillery.

The aircraft themselves were superbly designed to endure an air war fought at short range and low altitude. And no plane was more successful in this brutal environment than the famed Il-2 Shturmovik *(above)*, otherwise known as "the Flying Tank." So heavily armored was the burly, single-engined bomber that it was virtually immune to light-machine-gun fire as it battered German formations from altitudes of 300 feet or less. One Shturmovik survived 350 hits in the course of a dozen missions.

All told, an astonishing 36,163 Shturmoviks were built during the War, making it by far the most numerous Soviet combat aircraft. Nevertheless, a number of other bombers *(following pages)* played an important supporting role in the Soviet Air Force. Though less heavily armored than the Shturmovik, the Pe-2 had the advantage of twin engines, higher speed and greater maneuverability. A second twin-engined craft, the Il-4, was the first Soviet bomber intended to carry the air war far behind German lines, but its relatively light defensive armament eventually relegated it to antishipping missions along the Baltic coast.

Toward the end of the War, the swift, powerful Tu-2 came into service, both as a panzer buster and as a destroyer of targets deep inside Germany. The Soviets built only one plane that could be considered a long-range heavy bomber on the order of the U.S. B-17. It was the four-engined Pe-8, but high-level strategic bombing was not the mission of the Soviet Air Force in those days, and only 79 of the craft were ever produced.

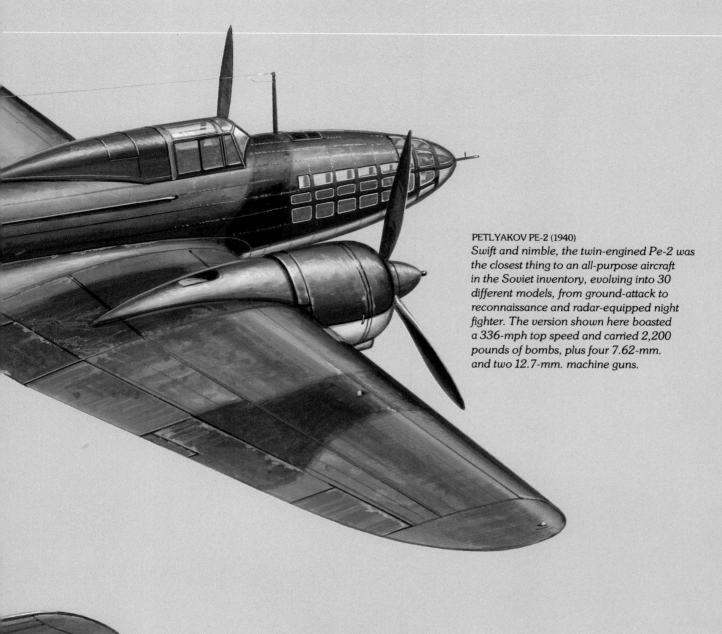

PETLYAKOV PE-2 (1940)
Swift and nimble, the twin-engined Pe-2 was the closest thing to an all-purpose aircraft in the Soviet inventory, evolving into 30 different models, from ground-attack to reconnaissance and radar-equipped night fighter. The version shown here boasted a 336-mph top speed and carried 2,200 pounds of bombs, plus four 7.62-mm. and two 12.7-mm. machine guns.

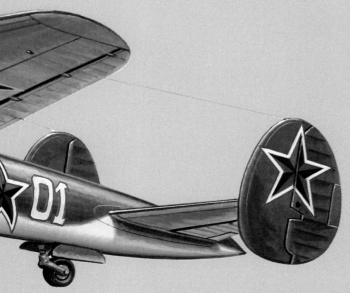

ILYUSHIN IL-4/DB-3F (1938)
The first Soviet plane to bomb Berlin, in 1941, the twin-engined Il-4 medium bomber could deliver a 2,204-pound payload to a target almost 1,200 miles away. But it quickly became obsolescent because of its slow (277 mph) speed and weak (only three machine guns) defensive armament. Many Il-4s were refitted to carry a one-ton aerial torpedo or a sea mine.

TUPOLEV TU-2 (1943)
Powered by two huge 1,850-hp engines, the Tu-2 medium bomber made its debut in 1943 as a successor to the Il-4. It featured an impressive 340-mph top speed, 2,200-pound payload and 1,305-mile range. This ground-attack version, manned by a crew of four, was armed with two 20-mm. cannon and three 12.7-mm. machine guns.

PETLYAKOV PE-8/TB-7 (1943)
The only Soviet heavy bomber to serve in the War, the four-engined Pe-8 could carry almost 8,800 pounds of bombs 2,920 miles to hit targets in Germany and the Balkans. But its main role was as a long-range VIP transport, most notably in 1942 when it flew diplomats from Moscow to London and Washington for lend-lease talks.

POLIKARPOV I-153 (1927)
A vulnerable anachronism in an age of monoplanes, the gull-winged I-153 was the last biplane fighter ever sent into combat by a major air force. Underpowered (1,000 hp, 280-mph speed) and undergunned (four 7.62-mm. machine guns), the I-153 did have the virtue of excellent maneuverability—but not enough to compensate for its flaws.

POLIKARPOV I-16 (1933)
This ski-equipped version of the I-16 had a 1,000-hp engine and a top speed of 304 mph. Its armament consisted of two 7.62-mm. machine guns and two 20-mm. cannon. Small bombs or rockets were carried on racks under the wings. A few I-16s were even fitted with special steel propellers for ramming enemy bombers.

A fleet of fighters old and new

When the Germans invaded Russia in 1941, the Soviet fighter inventory was huge but obsolete. Most of the 4,000 so-called frontline fighters were I-153 biplanes *(above)* and stubby I-16 monoplanes *(left)* dating from the late 1920s and early 1930s. The MiG-3 *(overleaf)* was a more modern design; but it was lightly armed and slow at low altitudes.

Soon after the initial disasters, however, a new class of Soviet fighters *(following pages)* began appearing in growing numbers. Designed just before the War, these planes were rugged, simple to produce, and very fast and maneuverable. The La-5 had an engine twice as powerful as those of the planes it replaced and could outspeed the vaunted Me 109. The Yak-3, which weighed only 5,842 pounds, could outturn any German opponent. An American plane, the Bell P-39 Airacobra, was extremely fast below 16,000 feet and heavily armed, thus perfectly suited to the low-altitude combat of the Eastern Front.

YAKOVLEV YAK-3 (1943)
Making its debut at the Battle of Kursk in 1943, the Yak-3 soon proved itself to be the premier Soviet fighter and one of the best in the world, often compared to the British Spitfire. Powered by a 1,659-hp engine, it boasted a top speed of 410 mph and could easily outmaneuver German fighters at low altitude; it was armed with two 12.7-mm. machine guns and one 20-mm. cannon.

MIKOYAN-GUREVICH MiG-3 (1940)
A flawed design, the MiG-3 was too unstable and poorly armed (one 12.7-mm. and two 7.62-mm. machine guns) to compete successfully in the swirling, wrenching dogfights over the front. But it was extremely fast in a straight line (398 mph) and was capable of climbing to almost 40,000 feet; it eventually found its niche as a reconnaissance plane.

BELL P-39N AIRACOBRA (1941)
Spurned by U.S. pilots for its poor high-altitude performance, the American P-39—with a 370-mph top speed—was considered an excellent low-level dogfighter and ground-attack plane by the Soviets. The unusual location of the engine—behind the cockpit—made room for antitank weapons: one 37-mm. cannon, six machine guns and 500 pounds of bombs. The Russians received almost 5,000 P-39s as lend-lease aid from the U.S.

LAVOCHKIN LA-7 (1944)
The most advanced Soviet fighter of World War II, the La-7 was the Russian answer to the Focke-Wulf 190, pride of the Luftwaffe. The Lavochkin had an enormous 1,850-hp engine and improved streamlining that enabled it to reach a speed of 413 mph, only 5 mph slower than the Fw 190; it was armed with two rapid-firing 20-mm. cannon. The aircraft shown here was flown by Ivan Kozhedub, whose 62 victories made him the Red Air Force's top ace.

5
Pobyeda! Victory!

Two days after the stillness of death had descended upon Stalingrad, a Red Army assault force landed at the foot of Mount Myskhako just southwest of the port city of Novorossisk on the Taman Peninsula. There, on the 4th of February, 1943, in an event neither widely noted nor long remembered amid the tumult of global war, the Soviets seized a 19-square-mile patch of German-held territory—and in so doing they triggered one of history's great aerial conflicts.

During that battle—which took its name from the Kuban River, flowing westward through swampy lowlands near the peninsula's northern perimeter—Russian and German planes clashed by the hundreds, screaming and swirling and tumbling through the sky in encounters that, as the weeks passed, became too numerous to count. On the ground, the Kuban was a slow, slogging affair that ended in stalemate. But in the air it was undeniably a Soviet victory, and the manner of its accomplishment was to be of enormous significance during the two years that remained of the Russo-German war. For the Red Air Force, the Kuban was a watershed. Always before, and even for most of the time at Stalingrad, its posture had been basically defensive. But no longer. In the springtime skies of the Kuban, Soviet airmen for the first time quickly seized the initiative, sending wave after wave of modern aircraft against the Luftwaffe in an aggressive prelude to the huge, skillfully coordinated air offensives that were to become the hallmark of the Red Air Force.

To be sure, the Soviets would still suffer setbacks. Dangerous almost to the end, the Luftwaffe would from time to time achieve at least temporary superiority over local battlefields. Nevertheless, the events that took place during the early months of 1943 were the first peals of thunder in the storm that would eventually sweep into the German homeland and bring to Berlin its Götterdämmerung.

Adolf Hitler could not for long abide the Soviet presence on the rocky beachhead at Mount Myskhako: It menaced Novorossisk, which in turn anchored his north-south defensive lines across the neck of the Taman Peninsula. That promontory was the German Army's sole remaining

Returning from a dogfight late in the War, Soviet ace Colonel Alexander Pokryshkin is congratulated by another officer. The stars on Pokryshkin's U.S.-built P-39 Airacobra tally his 55 kills to date.

foothold in the Caucasus. As such, it served not only as a buffer zone against Russian efforts to recapture the Crimea but as a potential spring-board from which his hopes for possessing the Caucasian oil fields might at last be realized.

For the remainder of the winter, weather hampered operations—and both sides used the respite to build their forces for the battle that was sure to come. By mid-April the German Army had amassed 400,000 troops in the Kuban region and the Luftwaffe's Air Fleet 4 could call upon more than 800 aircraft in the immediate vicinity, with another 200 available from the North Caucasus.

Meanwhile, the Soviet force at Myskhako had been strongly rein-forced by troops of the Eighteenth Army (whose top political officer was a colonel named Leonid I. Brezhnev), with about 800 planes of the Fourth and Fifth Air Armies deployed for action—and a great many more held in reserve.

In overall operational command of the two Soviet air armies was a general with a checkered past. At the outbreak of the Bolshevik Revolution, Konstantin A. Vershinin had left his work in a sawmill to enter the Red Army. In 1929, he was an experienced infantry of-ficer with a highly promising career presumably ahead of him. At that point—against his wishes and in spite of the fact that he had never flown—he was summarily assigned to the faculty of the Zhukov-sky Air Force Academy in Moscow.

Vershinin was evidently a natural flier: Quickly qualifying in every type of plane then possessed by the Soviet Air Force, he was promoted to colonel at the age of 38. Then, in August 1938, came a sudden and severe setback. Ordered to lead a flight of bombers to participate in a Moscow air exercise, Vershinin took off in foul weather—and five of the bombers crashed during the flight. Vershinin was court-martialed, re-duced in rank and sent to a new post.

Four months later, as Stalin's military purges reached their peak, Vershinin was understandably alarmed to receive a telegram from Moscow instructing him to "return at once." To his vast relief, he was told that because of an increasingly urgent need for quali-fied airmen he was being restored to his former post as a supervisor of advanced pilot-training programs.

Shortly after the German invasion of Russia, Vershinin was again discomfited by a summons to Moscow. This time he took the precaution of placing a telephone call to an old friend, General Pavel Zhigarev, now commanding the Soviet Air Force. "The Politburo and the High Com-mand," declared Zhigarev, "have named you commander of the air forces of the Southern Front. Congratulations."

Small comfort. All three of Vershinin's immediate predecessors in that particular post had already fallen into deep disgrace—and within a month would be dead at the hands of NKVD firing squads. Vershinin apparently was both luckier and more skillful than his unfortunate com-rades. He served well enough on the Southern Front to be offered a

Zeroing in on the smoke from earlier bomb hits, a squadron of Shturmoviks swoops down on German ground forces hidden in the Caucasus Mountains in 1943. The turbulent air currents and lofty peaks of the region were even more dangerous to the Soviet fliers than German antiaircraft fire.

series of other important commands, and was a lieutenant general early in 1943 when he returned to command the Fourth Air Army. But now the looming Kuban crisis offered a substantial prospect that the resurrected career of Konstantin Vershinin would come to a sudden halt.

The Germans struck from the air and on the ground at 6:30 on the morning of April 17 in an operation called *Neptune*—fittingly named, since its single-minded purpose was to shove the Soviet forces at Myskhako into the sea.

Even on that first day, the Luftwaffe appeared in the massive formations that were to become characteristic of the Kuban fighting: Approximately 450 bombers and 200 fighters flew more than 1,000 sorties, hammering time and again at Russian positions. Next day, despite heavy clouds, Air Fleet 4 was back with an assault that began at 4:45 a.m. and ceased only when twilight fell at 6:30 that evening. The results were discouraging: The German Seventeenth Army, while suffering severe losses, was able to dent the perimeter of the Soviet beachhead by little more than half a mile.

So far, the Red Air Force had responded sluggishly, suggesting the dreary possibility that it had reverted to its pre-Stalingrad ways. But the condition was more apparent than real. The Soviet air command was biding its time, declining to fritter away its strength while awaiting the arrival of three reserve corps—another 300 combat aircraft—that had been ordered to the Kuban. By April 20, the Soviets were ready to contend for dominion of the Kuban skies.

They came out early, they were full of fight and they hit hard. At 10 a.m.—just half an hour before the scheduled start of an all-out assault by German ground forces against the beleaguered Myskhako beachhead—a formation of 60 Soviet bombers, accompanied by 30 fighters, lashed at the Germans; they were closely followed by another wave, this one composed of 100 aircraft. Its timetable knocked askew from the start, the German Seventeenth Army was harassed throughout the day by fierce attacks from the sky, and nightfall found the Russian lines around Myskhako intact.

At dawn on April 21, both the Luftwaffe and the Red Air Force raised the ante, each striving desperately to attain superiority. Watching throughout the day from a command post near the village of Abinskaya, General Vershinin estimated that he saw a plane fall to its death on an average of once every 10 minutes.

Similarly, General Alexander Novikov, who had come to the Kuban as the High Command's representative, visited a forward command post and was eyewitness to a memorable dogfight. Flying an Il-2 Shturmovik without fighter escort, Lieutenant N. V. Rykhlin was suddenly jumped from above by four German fighters. In the wild scramble that followed, Rykhlin and his rear gunner shot down two of the enemy planes. Although Rykhlin was wounded and his Shturmovik was crippled, he landed safely at a nearby airfield—where both he and his gunner were immediately given battlefield promotions by the commander in chief of the Soviet Air Force.

On April 24, the Germans stopped trying to dislodge the Red Army from Myskhako and braced themselves against a Russian offensive aimed at smashing their main lines and driving them from the Taman Peninsula. It began at 7:40 on the morning of April 29 with a savage three-hour onslaught by 144 Soviet bombers, 82 ground-attack planes and 265 fighters against German positions around Krymskaya, a railroad junction northwest of Novorossisk.

Then and thereafter, the Luftwaffe resisted furiously, and for seven flaming weeks German and Russian fliers fought by day and by night for mastery of the airspace over the Kuban. One-on-one dogfights acted as magnets, attracting other planes from the crowded skies and escalating into melees. "First," recalled a Soviet fighter pilot, "a diving Me 109 would trigger an attack by a Yak, which in turn drew into battle the intended victim's wingman. In a short time a LaGG appeared, quickly followed by a P-39 Cobra." Within minutes, as many as 100 planes could find themselves embroiled amid "the flash of tracers, the rattle of machine-gun fire, flak bursts and the wild intermingling of aircraft at various altitudes."

Yet out of the hurly-burly certain individuals emerged as pilots of exceptional talent. On April 29, for example, Lieutenant Dmitri Glinka, a bushy-browed Ukrainian, led a group of six U.S.-made P-39 fighters in an attack on a formation of 60 Ju 88 bombers over Krymskaya. In the affray that followed, Glinka shot down three bombers. During the entire period of the Kuban fighting, he was credited with 21 kills (his brother Boris scored 10) and was well on his way toward the 50 that by War's end made him the fourth-ranking ace in the Soviet Air Force.

The brothers Glinka were by no means alone in distinguishing themselves: Alexander Pokryshkin, by now widely recognized as a tactical innovator of rare talent, was one of two pilots with 20 Kuban victories, and at least nine others downed 10 or more Luftwaffe planes.

Such numbers told much about the Russo-German air conflict as compared with the war in the West, where pilots compiled considerably more modest statistics. Not only did the low-altitude tactics required for close ground support diminish room for maneuver and result in high rates of attrition, but the airmen who fought in Russia, far from being rotated for intervals of rest, were routinely kept in almost continuous action for weeks or even months at a time. And during those periods of sustained combat they had abundant opportunities to score kills.

Strangely, success in the Kuban air bore little relationship to advances on the Kuban ground. Although the Soviets had by now established air superiority, their Fifty-sixth Army was making little headway. Krymskaya finally fell on May 4 after a total forward movement of only six miles on a 16-mile-wide front, and not until May 26 did the Russians renew their offensive.

When it came, the drive was preceded by the sort of aerial bombardment that would subsequently become standard for the Soviet Air Force. Starting at 6:30 a.m. and continuing for three hours, Russian planes attempted to blast open a four-mile-wide breakthrough corridor for Soviet troops and tanks. With 150 fighters providing cover, a first wave of 84 bombers plastered the area with high explosives; then, succeeding waves of 36 and 49 Shturmoviks skimmed the treetops to attack German positions at point-blank range. Finally, as the Soviet ground forces began to advance, Shturmoviks were used for the first time to lay down a concealing screen of smoke.

It was no use. After gains of two to three miles, the Soviet Army was fought to a standstill—and there it remained, unable to move and watching helplessly as the air battle continued overhead in unabated intensity, with the Red Air Force ultimately getting the best of it.

The claims of both sides were probably exaggerated. According to Soviet sources, the Red Air Force flew 35,000 sorties during the Kuban fighting and destroyed 1,100 German aircraft—more than the number the Luftwaffe had started with. Of their own losses, the Soviets said only that they were "considerably less." The Germans disputed the Soviets with a massive claim of 2,280 enemy planes destroyed. Yet on June 7, when the War drifted away from the Kuban and the Soviet military council for the area issued a victory statement, not even the most blatant German propagandist cared to dispute it.

By then, vast forces were gathering to the north, where the Germans were preparing to launch their third summer offensive—and the Soviets were baiting a trap.

Of the whole bloody pageant that was the Russo-German war, the surreal struggle that raged around—and above—the city of Kursk was the most fantastic. History would mark the Battle of Kursk as a mammoth collision of tanks. And so it was. Yet it was also the scene for fulfillment of Soviet military doctrine, which required orchestrated operations by air, armor, artillery and infantry, and in which the triumph of one was the triumph of all. After Kursk, although a frightful cost was yet to be exacted, the combined arms of the Soviet Union would move remorselessly toward an outcome that had, in fact, already been determined.

Given the condition of his forces and the demands made on his resources by other fronts, Hitler's plans for Russia in 1943 were limited—and realistic. Post-Stalingrad fighting had left a huge Soviet-occupied bulge near the center of the long front line. Extending westward for about 100 miles, with Kursk at its heart, the salient was 150 miles wide at its base. With a prewar population of 120,000, the city itself was unremarkable except for having given its name to a regional magnetic anomaly that rendered compasses virtually useless.

In the offensive code-named *Citadel,* the Germans had nothing more ambitious in mind than to stabilize their front line by choking off the neck of the salient, thereby bagging a very large lot of Soviet

With flames shooting from the muzzles of its twin 37-mm. cannon, an Il-2 Shturmovik roars in to hammer German positions during the Battle of Kursk in July 1943. Almost 1,000 ground-attack planes saw action in this pivotal campaign.

troops and equipment. That endeavor, originally scheduled for May, was postponed because of Hitler's desire to bring into action his new Tiger and Panther tanks.

Despite *Citadel's* modest aims, German preparations were as thorough as ever. Among other things, the Luftwaffe embarked on an extensive program of forward airfield construction carefully timed to accommodate the staggered arrival of combat units called from Germany, Norway and France, and from other parts of the Eastern Front. By the time the build-up was complete, Air Fleet 4, located in the Belgorod-Kharkov area south of the salient, had about 1,100 aircraft, while Air Fleet 6, around Orel to the north, had 730.

Incredibly, the Russians were privy to just about everything done or even planned by the enemy—thanks to the extraordinary efforts of Rudolph Rössler, code-named Lucy, a Soviet spy whose sources of information extended into the German High Command.

Forewarned was forearmed on a scale hitherto unknown in human conflict. Within the Kursk bulge the Soviets crammed 1.3 million troops, 20,000 guns and mortars, 3,600 tanks and self-propelled guns, and 2,900 aircraft—1,060 fighters, 940 ground-attack planes, 500 day bombers and 400 night bombers—mostly belonging to the Second and Sixteenth Air Armies.

But Russian plans went far beyond a mere defense of the salient: Poised on a north-south line across the neck of the Kursk protuberance was an enormous reserve, ready to lunge against the German flanks in the first phase of a general Soviet offensive. In all, General Novikov would have at his beck the power of six air armies totaling 5,400 planes.

On July 1, Hitler instructed his commanders to attack four days later. By nightfall, Lucy had informed the Russians of the decision. The stage was set, the cast was assembled, the actors were rehearsed—and the Soviet Air Force botched its opening lines.

At 3:15 on the balmy morning of July 5, some 1,000 engines throbbed as German pilots prepared to depart from five airfields around Kharkov to lend their explosive striking power to the weight of panzers in *Citadel's* first paralyzing blow. Before the pilots could take to the air, however, monitors detected a surge in Russian radio transmissions, and moments later radar reported that Soviet planes were approaching in hordes.

They were indeed. In a preemptive effort to cripple the Luftwaffe before *Citadel* could get fairly under way, the Soviet air command had sent more than 400 Pe-2s, Il-2 Shturmoviks, Yak-9s, Yak-1s and La-5s against the Kharkov airfields.

Taxiing through the assembled ranks of bombers in their scramble to take off, 200 Messerschmitt 109s swarmed into the sky, climbing rapidly to 10,000 feet. As the lower-flying Soviet armada appeared out of dawn's gray haze, the German fighters swept down. With the Luftwaffe holding the advantages of both altitude and surprise, the result was a slaughter. "It was a rare spectacle," recalled a Luftwaffe commander. "Everywhere planes were burning and crashing." Within the next few minutes, an estimated 70 Soviet planes were shot down, surviving formations were dispersed and the Russian attack was shattered at virtually no cost to the Germans.

For their rashly conceived and clumsily executed foray the Soviets would pay dearly on that fiery July 5. They had committed a significant proportion of their southern sector's fighter strength to the enterprise; now, as panzer spearheads slashed at Russian lines, few of the planes that had participated in the raid were fit to contest the clouds of attacking Luftwaffe aircraft. In the north, for reasons that remain obscure, the Soviet air response was equally torpid. All in all, Novikov had no cause to be pleased—and he demonstrated his dissatisfaction by removing a number of high-ranking officers.

Next day, Soviet air resistance stiffened somewhat, and on July 7, with the gigantic strikes that decimated 13 German panzer divisions, the numerical superiority held by the Russians began to assert itself. Against the throngs of German tanks now battering at Soviet ground positions, the Shturmoviks especially were in their element. Equipped with hollow-charge antitank bombs, the Shturmoviks took a terrible toll.

"We usually tried to attack from the rear," wrote Shturmovik pilot Alexander Yefimov, "where the armor was thinner and where the most vulnerable components of the vehicles were located: the engines and gas tanks." He added that "the effect was staggering as Hitler's celebrated Tigers burned under the strikes."

By now, the Shturmovik pilots had adopted tactics flexible enough to meet varying situations. Against panzers concentrated in combat formations, the Il-2s, usually flying in groups of eight to 12, deployed in the so-called circle of death. But against tanks in column on their way to combat, the Shturmoviks attacked either straight on or with S turns. Either way, Yefimov observed with clinical interest, "the greatest effect was achieved by using antitank bombs dropped from an altitude of 100-150 meters."

Shturmoviks, along with twin-engined bombers and strafing fighters, were also employed against the airfields from which the Luftwaffe was flying to the embattled salient, and Yefimov recalled one such attack, undertaken at dawn, with immense satisfaction. "The Hitlerites were not expecting our raid," he wrote. "The airfield was just beginning to stir. There were aircraft packed close together on the hardstands." Coming in low, Yefimov continued, the Soviet formation "dropped delayed-action bombs directly on the fascist bombers. A few seconds later, there was a powerful explosion. The enemy aircraft were burning. The airfield was shrouded in black smoke."

Because such missions involved relatively long distances, the Kursk region, with its faceless landscape and the freakish magnetic condition that distorted compasses, presented a special hazard. "Sometimes, upon returning from a mission," wrote Yak-9 pilot Sergei D.

Supporting artillery on the ground, Il-2 Shturmoviks skim over the Kursk battlefield in July 1943. The "peleng" formation shown here—with planes abreast in a staggered line—was a favored flying style in ground-attack sorties; it enabled aircraft to peel off easily to form an attack circle.

Luganskii, "we would circle a long time over the steppe, trying to search out our airfield. We'd fly farther, circle about, look around. Steppe and more steppe. You'd burn for some way out of this mess, and the terrain would remain completely unfamiliar. It was impossible to orientate yourself by compass—the effects of the Kursk magnetic anomaly. What the hell should I do?"

On one perplexing occasion, Luganskii spotted an infantry column marching below. "With some difficulty trying to keep the plane in a horizontal position," he recalled, "I ripped off a scrap of paper and scribbled on it with a pencil: 'Where's Novyi Oskol? Show me.' I then crumpled the paper in a mitten, flew over the heads of the infantrymen and threw the mitten on the ground. The infantrymen pounced on the mitten. Soon dozens of hands were pointing out the way to the proper route."

By July 9, with Novikov calling freely on his reserves, the Soviet Air Force was clearly in the ascendancy: For example, on the opening day of the battle the Luftwaffe had mounted 2,800 sorties over an area 25 miles wide and only seven miles deep in the Orel sector. Now it was down to 350 sorties, while the corresponding Soviet statistic had soared to well over 1,000.

For fighter pilots, the heavy Kursk traffic provided glorious opportunities. Flying a Yak-9, Lieutenant Alexei Gorovets was credited with nine kills during a singlehanded attack on a flight of 20 Stukas; however, Gorovets himself did not survive to tell of his astounding feat. Almost as noteworthy were the exploits of Alexei Maresyev, an La-5 pilot who destroyed five enemy planes in two days—despite the fact that he had lost both legs when shot down early in the War and was now flying with artificial limbs (*page 155*).

All but unnoticed amid the general carnage was the inconspicuous victory scored by a 23-year-old La-5 pilot of peasant background named Ivan Kozhedub. Flying a dawn sweep, Kozhedub's La-5 squadron encountered a flight of 20 Ju 87s crossing the front lines with fighter escort. In the swirling fight that followed, Kozhedub got on a Stuka's tail and began blazing away. Nothing happened. Kozhedub kept firing. Still nothing. Finally, his ammunition almost expended, Kozhedub considered ramming the enemy. Just then, the Stuka began trailing smoke—and soon plunged out of control to the earth. It was hardly a fancy kill, but it was the first of the 62 that would by War's end make Ivan Kozhedub the Soviet Union's leading ace.

On July 12, the Battle of Kursk came to a crescendo near the village of Prokhorovka, where more than 1,400 tanks clashed in savage hull-to-hull fighting that began at dawn and concluded beneath the moon's wan light. To the pilots who waged war in the smoke-filled sky above the battlefield, the day was as bewildering as it was deadly.

"The sky is full of planes," wrote a Yak pilot, reliving the memory as if it were present reality. "Messerschmitts and Lavochkins, Focke-Wulfs and Yakovlevs, Ilyushins and Junkers, Petlyakovs and Heinkels." After diving into a dogfight with a flight of Ju 88s, the pilot recalled that the enemy planes "rushed by so close to me from the right and from the left that it seemed I exchanged glances with the pilot of one of them. The side gunners didn't have a chance to open fire. It seemed that they, as well as we, were in such a situation for the first time and weren't sure right away what to do." "It was terrifying," said another Soviet fighter pilot. "German and Soviet fighters were whirling and diving everywhere. You would be involved in a fight with another aircraft and a couple of dogfights would be taking place in between yours. The risks of collision were enormous."

With both sides throwing in every resource available, the battle at Prokhorovka had so far been inconclusive, both on the ground and in the air, and both sides awaited renewal on the morrow. It never occurred: On July 13, Adolf Hitler, concerned by the Allied invasion of Sicily and the need to redeploy German troops there, declared that Operation *Citadel* was canceled.

After the German disengagement from Kursk, the dam burst. Everything went according to the High Command's plan; first, the Russians carried out a strong defense, followed immediately by an even stronger counteroffensive. Orel and Kharkov, the staging points for *Citadel,* fell to the Soviets in August. On November 6, the ancient Russian capital of Kiev passed back into Soviet hands, and in December Red Army forces sealed off the Crimea. By the end of 1943, nearly 390,000 square miles of Russian territory had been reclaimed by its owners.

In every sense, 1944 was the year of the avalanche. Rolling irresistibly on broad fronts, Soviet forces brought relief at last to long-suffering Leningrad, swept across the Crimea and smashed everything that stood in their path while clearing the Ukraine. By May, the only major tract of Russian territory remaining to the Germans was Belorussia, an immense and forbidding expanse of marshy lowlands, peat bogs, forests and lakes between the Ukraine and the Baltic states. The attempt to retake Belorussia was code-named *Bagration*—after a czarist general who led Russian troops during the Napoleonic wars.

With the June date for *Bagration* nearing, and with the Soviet factories now producing 3,300 planes a month, air commanders had at their disposal 13,428 mostly modern machines, including 8,798 combat aircraft assigned to frontline armies. Also appearing on the awesome inventory were 10,862 planes of American design and manufacture, shipped at much sacrifice to the Soviet Union as part of the lend-lease program begun in 1941.

Considering American generosity, it was savagely ironic that on the very eve of Operation *Bagration* there should befall the U.S. Army Air Forces one of the worst disasters it would suffer during the entire War—the result, at best, of Soviet negligence and at worst of the Kremlin's connivance.

From the start, the relationship between the Soviet Union and the United States had been a prickly one. And lend-lease, far from being a balm, had acted as an abrasive. The Soviet appetite for increased shipments was insatiable, complaints were constant and official criticism of American aircraft quality was unending.

There was, to be sure, some justice in the Soviet attitude. Thanks in part to a clumsy bureaucracy, the lend-lease effort had got off to a woefully slow start: By the end of 1942, only 1,440 aircraft had as yet arrived of the vast number—18,588 in all—that would reach the Red Air Force by the end of the War. Moreover, because of the bugs that were inevitable as U.S. industry strained to meet global demands, many of the planes sent to the Soviet Union in the early stages of lend-lease were defective. For example, the first Curtiss P-40 Tomahawks sent to Russia had faulty generators and had been shipped without spare parts.

But other aircraft were of great use, notably the Douglas A-20 Havoc, a swift, twin-engined light bomber superior to anything in the Soviet inventory; more than 2,900 A-20s were delivered. Another star performer for the Soviets was the Bell P-39 Airacobra, 4,746 of which were sent to the Red Air Force, plus another 2,402 advanced P-63 King Cobras. These two planes in particular were almost ideally suited to the Eastern Front. Sturdy, simple to fly, swift and maneuverable, they were equipped with 37-millimeter cannon fired through the propeller hub. Russian pilots who flew the plane—among them Alexander Pokryshkin—fondly called it *britchik,* or "little shaver."

It was against this background that the United States, late in 1943, officially requested that it be allowed to use Soviet airfields to conduct bombing raids against Germany and the enemy-occupied nations of Eastern Europe. The need was real: Flying round trips out of Great Britain and Italy meant that U.S. bombers were vulnerable to Luftwaffe attacks for prolonged periods; use of Russian bases, much closer to the targets, would save both lives and equipment.

Stalin hemmed and hawed for months, and it was not until March 1944 that he finally gave his agreement. Even then, he imposed severe restrictions. Instead of the six bases requested by the Americans, he would permit them to use three—at Poltava, Mirgorod and Piryatin, all in the Kiev area of the Ukraine. Instead of 2,100 ground personnel, only 1,200 Americans would be allowed to enter the Soviet Union. Targets for the U.S. bombers would be selected not by American commanders but by the Soviets. And Russian fighters would be responsible for airfield security; American planes would not even be allowed to participate.

At 2:24 on the afternoon of June 2, 1944, the first of 64 B-17 Flying Fortresses from bases in Italy touched down on the rain-spattered runway at Poltava after bombing German railroad-marshaling yards at Debrecen, Hungary, on the way. A little later, 65 other Fortresses landed at Mirgorod, while 64 P-51 fighter escorts touched down at Piryatin.

A gallery of heroic aces

One measure of the fantastic strength displayed by the reborn Red Air Force was the number of aces in its ranks. By War's end, more than 200 Soviet fliers claimed 20 or more German planes; 50 pilots had scored 30 or more victories, and 895 airmen had been decorated as Heroes of the Soviet Union, the supreme award for valor. Indeed, the top two aces, Major Ivan Kozhedub (62 kills) and Colonel Alexander Pokryshkin (59), won the Hero's gold medal three times.

Kozhedub set the Soviet record despite missing half the War. A brilliant instructor, he was held back from combat until July 1943, then was sent to the fray at the Battle of Kursk. At one point he scored an astonishing 11 victories in 10 days. For each victory, according to Soviet custom, a small red star was painted on his plane.

Lower-scoring aces became Heroes through pure grit. Some, like Senior Lieutenant Mikhail Baranov (24 kills), who plunged his damaged plane into an enemy tank column, martyred themselves for the Motherland. Others overcame enormous obstacles. One such man was Major Alexei Maresyev (19 kills), whose feet were crushed when he was forced to crash-land behind enemy lines. For 19 days Maresyev crawled in agony through the snow, subsisting on ants, berries and hedgehogs. Finally rescued, he lost both legs in surgery. A year later, Maresyev was back in the cockpit of a fighter. Seven more German planes fell to his guns.

Soviet aces (from left) Andreii Trud, Alexander Pokryshkin, Grigory Rechkalov and Nikolai Gulayev boasted a total of 198 kills.

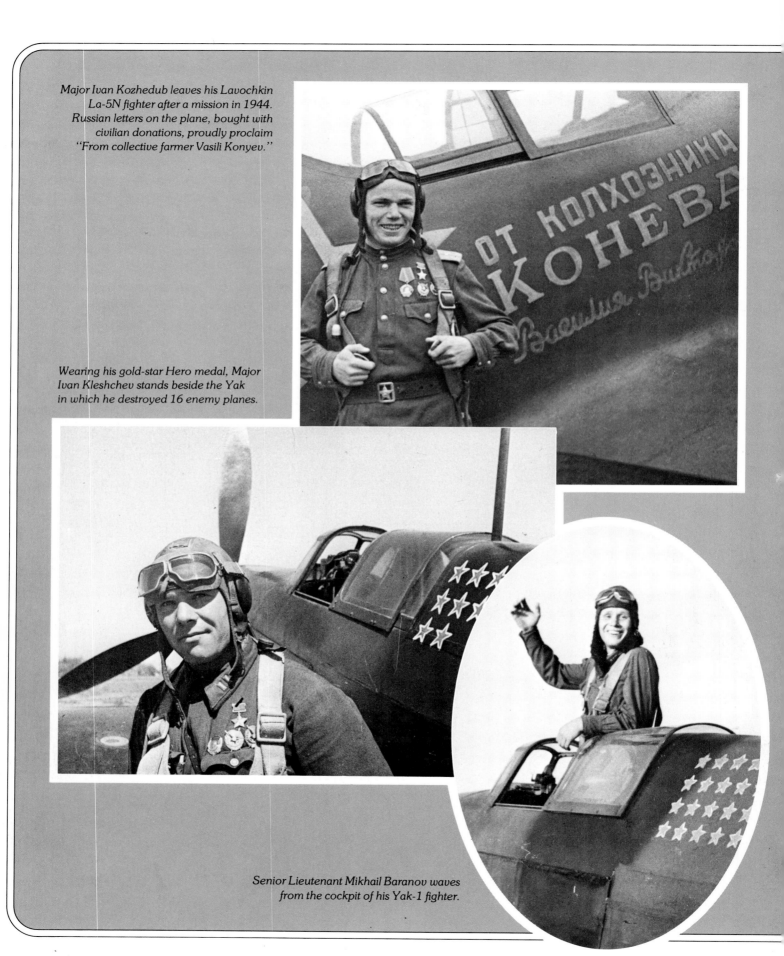

Major Ivan Kozhedub leaves his Lavochkin La-5N fighter after a mission in 1944. Russian letters on the plane, bought with civilian donations, proudly proclaim "From collective farmer Vasili Konyev."

Wearing his gold-star Hero medal, Major Ivan Kleshchev stands beside the Yak in which he destroyed 16 enemy planes.

Senior Lieutenant Mikhail Baranov waves from the cockpit of his Yak-1 fighter.

Commander Boris Safanov scored 22 kills in this British-built Hurricane.

Double amputee Alexei Maresyev, recovered from a long ordeal behind German lines, stands resolutely on his new artificial legs after resuming aerial combat.

A defender of Leningrad during its desperate siege of 1942, Major Pyotr Pokryshev gazes intently from the side of his American P-40E Warhawk. Fighting in 60 air battles, he amassed 22 victories and seven assists.

The Americans found their Soviet hosts to be entirely friendly. General Alexander Novikov even gave Lieutenant General Ira Eaker, the cigar-chomping U.S. commander, a tip on how to survive the endless toasts that were customary whenever airmen of the two nations got together: An apple eaten beforehand, confided Novikov, would absorb the vodka and enable even the most enthusiastic tippler to keep his feet.

By June 21, planes of the U.S. Fifteenth Air Force had carried out three raids. On that date, a huge force of about 2,500 bombers and fighters took off from England, heading toward Berlin. Shortly before reaching the German capital, 114 Fortresses and 70 P-51 Mustangs peeled away from the main group and bombed a synthetic-oil plant at Ruhland, 75 miles south of Berlin. Then the smaller group continued on to the Soviet airfields.

It had company. When reports from German ground stations indicated that the American planes were flying toward Russia, Luftwaffe commanders ordered a single Ju 88 to track them. Keeping a prudent distance, the Junkers followed the U.S. aircraft into the Soviet interior and watched while 73 of the B-17s landed at Poltava. Most of the American fighters put down at Piryatin, and the rest of the force went to Mirgorod.

That night, in ritual celebration of the successful U.S. raid, Americans exchanged toasts with their Russian hosts at Poltava. The amenities were still being observed when, at 11:35 p.m., a Russian soldier rushed in with a message for Poltava's Soviet commander, Major General A. R. Perminov, who informed his guests: "German aircraft have crossed Russian front lines and are headed toward this area." Air-raid sirens soon sounded. But Perminov did not seem unduly alarmed, and everyone remained in the mess hall. Again the Russian soldier appeared with a warning; again the signal was ignored, and not until a third message arrived did Perminov finally say: "I think we should go to the slit trenches."

Outside, the night was dark and silent—until, at 12:30 a.m., the throaty groan of aircraft engines sounded overhead and illumination flares, dropped from a German fleet of 80 Ju 88s and He 177s, bathed the night in a brilliant light. The 73 Flying Fortresses parked on the field stood out with stark clarity for the Luftwaffe airmen, who proceeded at a deliberate pace to cruise back and forth over the field, dropping no less than 110 tons of bombs. Finally, an American officer turned to his slit-trench companions: "Those damn bombers have been flying around overhead for more than an hour," he said. "Where the hell is the Red Air Force?"

Where indeed? Not a single Soviet plane had risen against the invaders. Moreover, when American commanders requested that the U.S. Mustangs at Piryatin be allowed to challenge the enemy bombers, permission was flatly denied by Soviet officials.

At 1:45 a.m., the bombing ceased—but the enemy aircraft still circled overhead. And then, at 2 o'clock, they attacked again, this time at

Demolished U.S. B-17s litter an airfield in the Ukraine in June 1944, victims of a Luftwaffe raid that destroyed 47 of the visiting American bombers.

low levels, with Ju 88s making repeated runs with antipersonnel bombs and machine-gun fire. The murderous assault lasted for 20 minutes, until at last the Germans departed. They left entirely unscathed. To the very end, not one Allied plane had flown against them. And on the field at Poltava, 47 Flying Fortresses lay in flaming ruins.

To the U.S. officers and men who had helplessly suffered the ordeal, the notion that a large number of German planes could inadvertently have been permitted to penetrate more than 300 miles was inconceivable. They were appalled by the failure of the Soviet defenders. A number of U.S. officers concluded that Stalin was determined to get rid of his unwanted guests. Clearly, for some Americans, the Cold War had already begun.

But before the implications had time to sink in, the events at Poltava were overtaken by the commencement of Operation *Bagration*.

It began three years to the day after German men and machines had crossed the Soviet frontier in what they confidently expected to be a lightning conquest. Now their bones and hulls and airframes littered the Russian landscape. And *Bagration* was simply overwhelming.

Flying in support of three Soviet army groups were the veteran First, Fourth and Sixteenth Air Armies, along with elements of the Third and Sixth Air Armies. In all, the Red Air Force had amassed more than 6,000 planes for the offensive, which would once and for all drive Hitler's minions from Soviet soil. Against that host, the Luftwaffe had pitiably little to offer: Operating for months without a reserve, it had been sorely afflicted by the attrition of the Kuban and Kursk, and it was even further enfeebled by the wholesale detachment of units to the West, where American and British forces had landed at Normandy on June 6. Now, on the entire Eastern Front, the Luftwaffe was down to 2,085 aircraft—including a paltry 395 fighters.

By June 25, with Soviet planes flying up to 5,000 sorties a day in pulverizing support, the Russian armies had crashed through German lines at several points, and the rout was on. Of the Soviet aircraft used in the offensive, fully one third were Shturmoviks, now in their glory. "With precise, low-altitude strikes," wrote Senior Lieutenant Yefimov, "they completely destroyed the fascists' concrete emplacements, smoked them out of their concrete pillboxes and, with cannon, rocket and machine-gun fire, destroyed Hitler's soldiers."

With the Luftwaffe virtually powerless, the Il-2s had more to fear from enemy ground fire than from German planes. While on a reconnaissance mission, wrote Yefimov, "our aircraft was taking hits from anti-aircraft guns, large-caliber machine guns, and tanks were firing at us. Evidently, everybody that had a gun was firing, because different-colored tracers were appearing ahead of, to the right, left and rear of the aircraft. I heard several direct hits."

Completing one run over enemy lines, Yefimov turned for a second. "The entire aircraft was again surrounded by smoke from the shell-

A jumble of wrecked Luftwaffe fighters, mostly frontline Fw 190s, lies on a hastily abandoned airfield near Berlin in the closing weeks of the War. In the foreground at right, a plane missing its engine has been cannibalized for desperately needed spare parts.

bursts. On the third pass, I went even lower. The fascists intensified their fire,'' he recalled. ''We flew along in a sea of fire, a little piece of hell. Fragments from the shells were beating along the aircraft. The seconds seemed like an eternity.''

When Yefimov landed safely back at his base, a mechanic ''counted over 200 large and small holes in the aircraft. The left wing was completely in tatters; only patches of the stabilizer were left.''

To all intents and purposes, the mission of Operation *Bagration* was accomplished by July 4: With losses of almost 300,000 men killed, wounded or captured, the German Army Group Center, which had led the 1941 march toward Moscow, no longer existed. By the end of August the Soviet homeland was completely liberated. The way to Poland and Germany itself lay before the Soviet juggernaut.

Warsaw fell on January 17, and the Soviet tide rolled on, reaching the Oder and Neisse Rivers by February 1. There, with advanced units only 38 miles east of Berlin, the Soviet armies stopped, presumably to consolidate their position and attend to the logistical problems of resupply and redeployment. During the lull, which later caused angry words among Soviet generals, other forces firmly established themselves in the Balkans.

Not until April 16 did the great lunge for Berlin commence. For that final battle of the Russo-German war, General Novikov had collected a gigantic force of 7,500 combat aircraft, whose operations he coordinated with a skill gained by hard experience. To oppose him, the Luftwaffe, using the respite granted by the 10-week Soviet delay, had managed to scrape together about 2,200 planes.

Early on the foggy morning of April 16, about 150 night bombers from the Fourth and Sixteenth Air Armies struck German positions on the west bank of the Oder while Russian artillery added its fire to the bombardment. In the northern sector, where the Oder is split into two branches by the marshy lowland that lies between, some ground units got bogged down almost immediately.

"Our fighting men cleared the enemy out of the area around the river while operating up to their waists in the swampy mud and by climbing onto the high spots and trees when the tide came into the mouth of the Oder from the Baltic Sea," explained an Il-2 pilot. "Naturally, under these conditions, neither the artillery nor the tanks were really able to assist."

The Shturmoviks came to the rescue with dispatch. "The vectoring stations," continued the airman, "provided us with precise coordinates of where the strikes should be delivered. At other times, our missions were provided after we were already airborne and, 5-10 minutes later fire rained down on the enemy, destroying his men and equipment." Eventually, he recalled, "things reached a point where, after expending all our ammunition—bombs, shells, rockets and machine-gun belts—we continued to fly over the battlefield at low altitudes, sowing panic and fear."

Farther south, the passage of Marshal Ivan Konev's First Ukrainian Army Group across the Neisse was eased by an air technique pioneered—with inconclusive results—during the Kuban fighting. A smoke screen, recalled Konev, "was laid toward the end of the first phase of the artillery preparation. As far as I could see, it was very successful—powerful, of good density and just the right altitude.

"It was laid skillfully by our assault planes. Flying at low altitude and high speed, they laid the smoke screen exactly on the bank of the Neisse. It must be mentioned that they had to lay the smoke screen along a front 390 kilometers long, no less and no more. It was very calm; wind velocity was only half a meter a second, and the smoke floated slowly over the enemy defenses, enveloping the entire Neisse Valley, which was what we needed."

With the crossings of the Oder and the Neisse, the last natural lines of defense for Berlin, time ran out for the Third Reich. During the fortnight that followed, the Red Air Force crowded so closely upon the dying city that the autobahns at Berlin's approaches were used as airstrips. In the orgy of killing and destruction, senses were numbed and memories were clouded.

On April 30, 1945, Adolf Hitler took his own life in his bunker amid the rubble of Berlin. And on May 1 a pair of Yak-3s, piloted by Major

A flight of Shturmoviks soars above a battered and burning Berlin on April 30, 1945, the day Soviet troops hoisted the Red banner over the Reichstag. The plane in the foreground is marked "Avenger."

I. A. Malinovsky and Captain K. V. Novoselov, screamed at 100 feet over the Spree River, which bisects Berlin, banked sharply over the ruins of the city and swept across the smoldering shell of the Reichstag. From the lead plane, banners unfurled and descended on the triumphant Soviet troops. Upon their red backgrounds a single word was embroidered in gold: *Pobyeda!* Victory!

To the victors, in a sense and on a scale hitherto beyond comprehension, belonged the spoils. And the carefully planned pillage that took place amid the ashes of the Third Reich would provide a modern foundation for the postwar Soviet Air Force.

Eighty per cent of the German aircraft industry, concentrated in the east to avoid Anglo-American strategic bombing, fell into Russian hands, along with designs, prototypes, experimental research, engines, machine tools, production stocks and a brilliant work force of scientists and engineers.

At the time of its defeat, Germany was leading the world in the development of jet aircraft and guided missiles—and the Soviet Air Force was still entirely equipped with piston-engined aircraft. Now, at the Junkers engine factory at Bernburg, the Russians found and appropriated the latest Jumo 004 turbojet engine and prototypes for improved design. At the Walter factory in Prague they acquired the newest Me 262 jet interceptor. At the Heinkel plant at Warnemund they discovered a light, inexpensive jet fighter already in production. At Focke-Wulf they got Professor Kurt Tank's designs for a jet interceptor and a second, rocket-powered fighter.

Some of Germany's best scientists were also gathered up, among them Gunther Bock, chief of research at the Experimental Aeronautics Institute; Messerschmitt's Rudolph Rental, the project engineer for the Me 163 and Me 263 rocket-powered fighters; Adolph Betz, a world authority on swept-wing design; Heinkel's senior designer, Siegfried Gunther; and Brunolf Baade, formerly chief designer for Junkers.

Offered security, good pay and accommodations, many Germans were perfectly willing to work for the Soviet Union. Meanwhile, NKVD agents combed the prisoner-of-war camps for scientific and technical personnel who might be of use and organized a ruthless hunt for those scientists known to have gone into hiding.

A representative of the Commissariat of Aviation described the scene that occurred when the Russians took over the huge Junkers plant at Dessau: "Individual dismantlers who were sent on a reconnaissance of the district encountered pleasant surprises everywhere. There were small factories, branches of Junkers and other firms, which were still working. In one small place on the banks of the Mulde they discovered a former paper factory, which was still engaged in the assembly of BMW airplane turbines, one of the latest jet engines at that time. Two stories of the factory building were filled with crates containing new turbines in perfect order.

"In Dessau the first Soviet truck with a group of dismantlers drove through empty streets. The town seemed dead. It was just the same in the Junkers factory. Except for two German guards there wasn't a soul in sight. All the equipment, with the exception of a few precision tools and instruments, was in the right place. It was possible to start work.

"The next day the news spread through the town that the Russians were starting up the factory again. The next piece of news astounded the Germans: The Russians were also giving jobs to leading specialists, notwithstanding their long record of membership in the National Socialist Party. One after the other, people 'with a name' began to turn up, happy that they were not looked at askance for having a party card."

In the autumn of 1946, the Kremlin decided that more efficient use could be made of the most skilled German technicians if they were employed at factories in Russia. On the night of October 21-22, the Soviets knocked on doors at thousands of homes, woke the occupants and told them to dress and pack. Entire families—along with anyone unfortunate enough to be visiting at the time—were scooped up by the dragnet and taken on special trains to Russia.

No accurate figures are available for the number of workers taken to Russia, but there were at least 3,000 and German estimates ranged as high as 300,000. And when they got there, the workers were bemused to find that their offices and workshops in Germany had been faithfully duplicated—right down to the ash trays and calendars.

The speed with which such methods enabled the Soviet Union to close the gap with the West in sophisticated military aviation became apparent to startled observers at the annual May Day display in Moscow in 1947. At the end of World War II, Russia still had not produced a successful jet engine. Now, less than two years later, the May Day flypast was led by formations of Yak and MiG jets, making their public appearance for the first time. Also making its debut was Russia's Tu-4 strategic bomber—which appeared strangely familiar to American eyes. In fact, it was a direct copy of U.S. B-29 Superfortresses that had made forced landings on Soviet territory after bombing Japan during the War, thereby presenting the Red Air Force with perfect examples of the world's most sophisticated bomber.

The display, like those that have followed, was deceptive in high degree. The basic strength of the modern Soviet Air Force rests not on stolen technology or second-hand ideas but on that titanic midcentury struggle in which the Russians, rising from the abyss, produced nearly 126,000 aircraft, flew more than 2.5 million sorties and claimed 77,000 German planes destroyed while losing more than 70,000 of their own.

From that searing experience emerged a formula in which great mass, immense sacrifice and an inflexible resolve to employ air power in close support of ground forces are the ingredients of *Pobyeda*. In their dedication to that doctrine, even under the umbrella of strategic bombers and intercontinental nuclear missiles, Soviet air commanders have never wavered.

A modern colossus with a global reach

For all its great size and strength, the Soviet Air Force that emerged victorious from World War II remained a relatively blunt instrument, limited in mission and unsophisticated in aircraft. But in the ensuing decades, as Soviet ambitions expanded, the Red Air Force underwent a dramatic change. By the early 1980s it had become an awesome, many-edged weapon that could project Soviet power at any time anywhere across the face of the globe.

Strategic bombing, once a monopoly of the West and particularly of the U.S. Air Force, may now be regarded as equally a Soviet specialty, with squadrons of supersonic bombers equipped for midair refueling and armed with long-range nuclear-tipped standoff missiles. By way of reconnaissance, flights of huge turboprop craft routinely make the 6,000-mile journey between Moscow and Cuba, gathering electronic intelligence all along the route.

In World War II, the only real Soviet airlift came from the twin-engined U.S. Douglas DC-3s assembled under license; in the 1980s, the Soviets boasted half a dozen types of jet and turboprop transports, including one monster that could haul 80 tons of weapons almost 7,000 miles. As for a naval air presence, by 1983 the Soviets had constructed four jet-and-helicopter carriers to challenge yet another patented U.S. strength.

None of this expansion of mission has been at the expense of what remains the primary Air Force task: air-combat superiority and close-in battlefield support. In the 1970s, no fewer than 15 different fighter and attack types were added to the inventory, as Soviet designers unceasingly worked to apply each new breakthrough and achieve qualitative parity with the West.

Nor have the Soviets faltered in their devout belief in numbers. At a time when a single jet fighter can cost upward of $30 million, the true measure of the Kremlin's investment in air power can be seen in the totals: 10,600 frontline military aircraft, among them 250 strategic bombers, 4,700 interceptors, 2,850 ground-attack planes, 1,200 attack helicopters, 600 heavy-lift transports. By comparison, the United States could count only 6,500 warplanes of all types.

At a Soviet air base, a squadron of pilots leaves the flight line after a practice mission in their MiG-23 fighter-bombers. Produced in half a dozen models, this highly advanced, 1,520-mph jet was the most versatile and numerous frontline Soviet combat aircraft of the early 1980s, with more than 2,000 planes in the Red Air Force inventory and another 500 supplied to satellite and client states.

Crewmen service a MiG-25 interceptor, known as "Foxbat" to NATO airmen. Developed in the late 1960s in response to a U.S. supersonic bomber prototype (the B-70) that never saw service, the twin-engined jet has a fantastic speed of 1,850 mph and a service ceiling of 80,000 feet. About 400 were built; for lack of anything to intercept, it has performed most successfully as a short-range reconnaissance craft.

Preparing for a night-training mission, a pilot boards an all-weather Su-15 interceptor equipped with a powerful nose-mounted radar. Though smaller and slower than the MiG-25, the missile-armed fighter boasts a 1,650-mph speed coupled with a spectacular climb rate of 45,000 feet per minute.

fly in tight formation during an Air Force aerobatic exercise. One of the earliest supersonic Soviet planes, the nimble little 1,385-mph craft was the premier fighter for the Red Air Force in the late 1960s and early 1970s; no fewer than 8,000 were produced in 17 models for service in 23 countries.

Camouflaged in sand and olive, a MiG-23 screams skyward with shock waves issuing from its afterburner. The wings sweep back for high speed

Vivid. . . . .
workhorse, a 1960s-vintage Tu-95 reconnaissance bomber flies over the North Atlantic in 1981, ignoring an escort of U.S. F-14 and British Sea Harrier jets from a nearby NATO task force. This particular model is equipped with a refueling probe that enables it to remain aloft for 28 hours.

A Tu-16 Badger—a onetime medium bomber converted to airborne tanker— extends a fuel-hose drogue to the nose of a rakish twin-engined Tu-22 bomber behind it. About 200 of the 1,000-mph Tu-22s were in service in the early 1980s, performing as strategic nuclear bombers, air-to-surface missile carriers and high-speed maritime reconnaissance craft.

A Tu-22M "Backfire" bomber takes off, swing wings extended for maximum lift. The craft can fly at 1,320 mph and has a 7,500-mile range.

An An-22 heavy turboprop transport, only slightly smaller than the U.S. DC-10 airliner, disgorges a rocket launcher from its rear bay. Approximately 55 of the huge 500,000-pound craft were in service in the early 1980s.

From clamshell doors in its belly, an Il-76 jet transport releases an armored personnel carrier to float earthward by parachute. At 13 tons apiece, three such vehicles can be carried in an Il-76, together with the men and gear to operate them.

Lined up after a massive airlift demonstration in 1971, a fleet of An-12 turboprops displays the 23-mm. tail guns the Soviets favor for their military transports. Each plane can carry 100 soldiers on folding seats along the walls and down the center—and disembark them in less than one minute through rear doors. An estimated 500 such craft were in service at the start of the 1980s.

On board the carrier Minsk off Japan in 1979, crewmen service three Yak-36 vertical-takeoff-and-landing fighter-bombers. Though less advanced